D0177285

Speaking Clearly

Student's Book

Speaking Clearly

Pronunciation and
Listening comprehension
for learners of English

Student's Book

Pamela Rogerson
Judy B. Gilbert

The right of the
University of Cambridge
to print and sell
all manner of books
was granted by
Henry VIII in 1534.
The University has printed
and published continuously
since 1584.

Cambridge University Press
Cambridge
New York   Port Chester
Melbourne   Sydney

Adapted from *Clear Speech* by Judy B. Gilbert
(Cambridge University Press, 1984)

Published by the Press Syndicate of the University of Cambridge
The Pitt Building, Trumpington Street, Cambridge CB2 1RP
40 West 20th Street, New York, NY 10011, USA
10 Stamford Road, Oakleigh, Melbourne 3166, Australia

© Cambridge University Press 1990

First published 1990

Printed in Great Britain by Bath Press, Avon

ISBN 0 521 31287 6 Student's Book
ISBN 0 521 31295 7 Teacher's Book
ISBN 0 521 32187 5 Set of 2 Cassettes

Copyright
It is normally necessary for written permission to be obtained
in advance from the publisher. However, the tests in *Speaking Clearly*
on pages 2–6 and 109–112, which carry the wording '© Cambridge
University Press 1990', may be photocopied. The usual requirement is
waived here and it is not necessary to write to Cambridge University
Press for permission.

CE

Contents

Contents

Acknowledgements

I would like to thank all my colleagues and friends at York
Language Training and Accès for their assistance and encouragement.
I am also very grateful to Alec Sabin and Radio Riviera for allowing
me to use their recordings.

P.R.

The authors and publishers are grateful to the following for
permission to reproduce material:
Warner Chappell Music Ltd for the extract from 'From The Air' by
Laurie Anderson on p. 44, © Difficult Music; Jeremy Pembrey for
the photographs on pp. 120–1, except for the photograph of the
painter which is from Barnaby's Picture Library.

Cartoons by Tony Hall. Artwork by Hilary Evans, Wenham Arts
and Peter Ducker.
Book design by Peter Ducker MSTD.

Introduction

When you are speaking a foreign language there are times when the other person does not understand you, or you do not understand the other person – we can call this a 'communication breakdown'.

Sometimes 'communication breakdown' is due to a grammar or vocabulary mistake and sometimes it is due to a pronunciation mistake. Just as you need to be able to analyse and correct your grammar and vocabulary mistakes you need to be able to analyse and correct your pronunciation mistakes.

It is not necessary to pronounce every sound perfectly to be understood – only a few parts of each sentence are really important, but these parts are essential. The native speaker depends on hearing these parts clearly, therefore you need to know which parts of a sentence must be clear and how to make them clear.

This book concentrates on elements of pronunciation which increase 'intelligibility', i.e. help you to understand and be understood in English.

⊡ marks the sections that are recorded on the cassettes.

PART 1: PRONUNCIATION

Name: .... Date: ....
Nationality: ....

Pronunciation test ⌑

The purpose of this test is to find which parts of English pronunciation may interfere with the way you understand and use spoken
English. How you **hear** English is closely connected with how you
speak English.

    This test is recorded on the cassette.

A

How many syllables (beats) are there in these words?
Example:
beauty = 2 (beau–ty)
beautiful = 3 (beau–ti–ful)

Now listen and write down the number of syllables you hear in each
word. You will hear each word twice.

1 open   ....   4 closed   ....
2 difficult   ....   5 variation   ....
3 taxes   ....

B

Which syllable is prominent or stressed in these words?
Example:
<u>Mon</u>day
to<u>mor</u>row
edu<u>ca</u>tion

Now listen and draw a line under the most strongly stressed syllable.
You will hear each word twice.

1 participant   4 photography
2 photograph   5 reliable
3 November

© Cambridge University Press 1990

C

Which syllables are not stressed (have weak sounds)?
Example:
ábout
atóm
átomíc

Now listen and draw a line through the weak sounds in each word.
You will hear each word twice.

1 banana   4 women
2 woman   5 Japan
3 Canada

D

Which word do you hear in these sentences?
Example:
So, your name is i) Lampert, is it? ....
               ii) Lambert   ....✗.....

Now listen and put a cross next to the word you hear:

1 That's i) **Miss, isn't it?** ....
       ii) **Ms (mizz)**   ....
2 And you live at 22 i) Rishley Road. ....
                   ii) Richley   ....
3 And your name, sir, is i) Vinney, is that right? ....
                   ii) Finney   ....
4 And the address is 15 i) Boot Street. ....
                  ii) Booth   ....
5 That's in i) Axbridge, isn't it? ....
      ii) Haxbridge   ....

© Cambridge University Press 1990

E

Is the rhythm of these phrases the same or different? Listen to this
example:

```
 •  —  •   —        •  —  •  —
```
Trafalgar Square   a cup of tea   'Same'

Now listen and decide if the the rhythm of the phrases on the left is
the **same** (write S) as or **different** (write D) from the phrases on the
right. You will hear each phrase once.

1 Oxford Circus	please be quiet	....
2 Richmond Road	hurry up	....
3 Victoria Station	a cup of tea	....
4 Leicester Square	answer the phone	....
5 Pall Mall	sit down	....

F

Dictation. What are the missing words in these phrases?
Example:
She .... go.   <u>can't</u>
He .... going.   <u>isn't</u>

Now listen and write in the missing words. You will hear each
sentence once.

 1 She doesn't .... to do it now.
 2 Please .... message.
 3 .... think she'll come?
 4 Where .... go?
 5 How .... you been here?
 6 .... busy?
 7 .... call her at six?
 8 What .... done?
 9 I'm afraid .... at the moment.
10 .... told me if he'd known.

     © Cambridge University Press 1990

G

Which word has the most stress (prominence) in each sentence?
Example:
That's a <u>great</u> idea.

Now listen to the dialogue. Underline the most stressed word in each sentence. You will hear the dialogue once only.

A: What's the matter?
B: I've lost my hat.
A: What kind of hat?
B: It was a rain hat.
A: What colour rain hat?
B: It was white. White with stripes.
A: There was a white hat with stripes in the car.
B: Which car?
A: The one I sold!

H

Can you recognise groups of words? Two identical sentences may have a different interpretation.
Example:
John said, 'My father is here.'
'John,' said my father, 'is here.'

Now listen to one sentence from each of the following pairs. Put a cross next to the sentence you hear. You will hear it twice.

1 a) Alfred said, 'The boss is stupid.'   ....
 b) 'Alfred,' said the boss, 'is stupid.'   ....

2 a) He sold his houseboat and motorbike.   ....
 b) He sold his house, boat and motorbike.   ....

3 a) If you finish, quickly leave the room.   ....
 b) If you finish quickly, leave the room.   ....

4 a) Pressing the pedal slowly, push the lever forward.   ....
 b) Pressing the pedal, slowly push the lever forward.   ....

5 a) The passengers, who had blue boarding cards,
   were told to board the plane.   ....
 b) The passengers who had blue boarding cards
   were told to board the plane.   ....

© Cambridge University Press 1990

5

I

The movement of our voice (pitch) can change the interpretation of sentences. Can you interpret the meaning of these sentences?
Example:
It was awful.   (statement)
It was awful.   (question)

Now listen to these sentences. Underline one of the two words or phrases in brackets that best interprets the meaning of each sentence. You will hear each sentence twice.

  1 She left her glasses.   (question / statement)
  2 He's finished.   (question / statement)
  3 The number is 35547.   (statement / contradiction)
  4 It's 22 Hills Road.   (statement / contradiction)
  5 You're English, aren't you? (fairly sure / not very sure)
  6 That's his sister, isn't it? (fairly sure / not very sure)
  7 Really.   (very interested / not very interested)
  8 Thanks.   (very interested / not very interested)
  9 I like the garden.   (enthusiastic / not very enthusiastic)
10 The kitchen is nice.   (enthusiastic / not very enthusiastic)

© Cambridge University Press 1990

1 Syllables

 The syllable is the basic unit of English pronunciation. Listen to the following words and notice how some of them have two or more parts or sounds.

one syllable	two syllables	three syllables
ease	easy	easily
will	willing	willingly

A

As you listen to the following words and phrases, count the number of syllables you hear.

one syllable	two syllables	three syllables	four syllables
I	seven	eleven	identity
my	eighteen	syllable	analysis
name	sentence	important	it's important
called	focus	emphasis	he wants a book
real	really	realise	reality

B

Say your name aloud and decide how many syllables there are in it. Do the same with the other members of the class.

C

Listen and practise saying these words, counting the syllables on your fingers. Be careful not to add or subtract syllables. Decide exactly how many syllables there are in the words in the third column.

one syllable	two syllables	three or more syllables
fun	funny	stupidly
sing	singer	sentences
write	writer	registration

>>>→

one syllable	two syllables	three or more syllables
wind	windy	difficult
blow	below	economy
prayed	parade	economical
loud	aloud	classify
sticks	stickers	establishment
tasks	attack	astronomical

D

Grammar mistakes are sometimes the result of not hearing the number of syllables. For example:
a) They've rent(ed) a house.
b) There are two dish(es).

1 Listen to the following words. Which have one syllable and which have two syllables?

painted	rented	added	caused
walked	worked	watched	started
landed	closed	folded	laughed

What is the rule? (See RULE CHECK on page 10.)

2 Listen to these sentences. Are they about the past or the present? Put a cross in the appropriate column.

	Past	Present

Example:
The talk last(ed) for hours.   ×

1 They start(ed) at 10.00.
2 We often rent(ed) a house on holiday.
3 They regularly visit(ed) the cathedral at Christmas.
4 The teachers want(ed) a pay rise.
5 I intend(ed) to go shopping on Saturday.

3 Listen to the following words. Which words have one syllable and which have two?

causes	dishes	watches	cakes
rules	files	misses	pieces
mixes	changes	loves	prices

What is the rule? (See RULE CHECK on page 10.)

4 Listen to the sentences on the recording and decide which of the
  two words you hear.
  Example: match / matches
  The matches fell on the floor.

  1 excuse / excuses
  2 beach / beaches
  3 finish / finishes
  4 box / boxes
  5 tax / taxes   increase / increases

E

Practise saying the following words and put them into the correct
column, according to the number of syllables.

starts	extra	sentences	mixed
completed	little	scream	interfaces
stopped	mixes	sport	taxes
manages	started	uses	communication
advantages	hopes	support	international
castle	pieces	managed	

one syllable	*two syllables*	*three syllables*	*four or more syllables*
....	....	....	....
....	....	....	....
....	....	....	....
....	....	....	....
....	....	....	....

F

Disappearing syllables. Sometimes in natural spoken English vowel
contractions cause syllables to 'disappear' completely.

  Look at these words. How many syllables would you expect in
each word? Write the number down. Listen to the words and write
down the number of syllables you actually hear.

	Expected number	*Actual number*
Example: medicine	3	2
1 chocolate	....	....
2 vegetable	....	....
3 comfortable	....	....
4 interesting	....	....
5 secretary	....	....
6 library	....	....

G 😑

Dictation. Listen to these sentences and write the words that are missing.

1 The .... lovely.
2 The plane .... at eight.
3 Petrol .... last month.
4 Did you .... the Mosque?
5 She put .... in the suitcase.
6 They .... car.
7 .... yesterday.

Check your progress 😑

1 Record yourself saying the following sentences several times. Then listen to the recording. Check the number of syllables very carefully. It is difficult to hear your own mistakes, but it is important.

   1 'Can I have six oranges and two pieces of cheese ... oh ... and three boxes of dates please, one large and two small.'

   Did you have three syllables for 'oranges', two for 'pieces' and 'boxes', and one for 'dates'?

   2 'This is the first city they visited when they travelled around the country, and they liked it very much.'

   Did you have two syllables for 'this is', 'city' and 'travelled', three syllables for 'visited' and one for 'liked'?

2 Now listen to the recorded extract of natural speech and write down what you hear.

Rule check

Rule 1

Regular past tense verbs that end in a 't' or 'd' sound in the basic form will add an extra syllable in the past tense.

Rule 2

Nouns and verbs ending in a hissing sound (i.e. a sibilant) have an extra syllable when an 's' is added.
Example: pass   buzz   box   church   change   dish

2 Stress

In English some syllables are much more prominent than others. This prominence, or stress, is important to make speech clear. There are three main signals of stress:

1 Pitch change
2 Length of syllable
3 Vowel quality

Together, these signals make syllables sound louder.

Pitch change

When we speak our voice moves up and down. That is, it changes pitch. Look at this word:

ba^{na}na

Which syllable has the highest pitch?

A

Listen to these words. Underline the syllable with the highest pitch.

quarter   admission
career   applicant
division   application
residence   education
requirements   information
professional

B

There are many words in English which are similar in other languages, but different syllables are stressed in different languages.

>>>→

Listen to these words. Which syllable has the highest pitch?
Example: <u>cho</u>colate

cafeteria	orange
service	algebra
telephone	biology
theory	minister
president	

Syllable length

In English, some syllables are long and some are short. Syllables are extra long when they are prominent.

C 📼

Listen to these names:

Barbara   Peter

Which syllable is the longest in each word?

D 📼

Listen and practise saying the following words, concentrating on the different duration (length in time) of the syllables.

— .	. —	. — .	— . .
statement	estate	solution	beautiful
Peter	repeat	tomato	easily
sign it	design	it's ready	open it
longer	along	he's busy	give me some

E 📼

Listen to these sentences and write down the words that are missing.

1 I hope you like it. I .... it ....
2 .... not here yet. He'll be .... in a
....
3 The .... agent was ....
4 Can you .... as soon as .... ?

Vowel quality

English has two kinds of vowels: strong and weak. The difference between strong and weak vowels is essential to the language. Stressed syllables *always* have strong vowels. Unstressed syllables *usually* have weak vowels.

Note: The weak vowels are the most commonly used vowels in English.

 Listen to this word:

banana

Now listen again and decide which syllable has the strong, clear vowel sound.

The word 'banana' has three letter 'a's, but only one 'a' is said with a strong, clear sound. The other two 'a's are said with a different, weak sound. This sound is very short.

bánaná   Canádá   dramá

F

Listen to the following words. Which syllables have weak vowels? Put a line through them.
Example: Décembér

November	January
July	September
August	April

G

Listen and then practise contrasting strong and weak vowels. Notice how the vowel changes from strong to weak (and vice versa) in the two columns.

pot	pótato
Tom	atóm
man	womán
men	womén
add	ádditión
office	óficiál

13

H ☐

Listen to the names of these cities. Underline the strong vowels.
Example: <u>A</u>thens

one strong vowel
Paris
Madras
Caracas
Manila
Ottawa
Milan

two strong vowels
Philadelphia
Casablanca
Stockholm
Hong Kong
Copenhagen

Note: Some strong vowels are not stressed.
Example:

AIRport   shamPOO
INdex   PREsent (noun)
PASSport   presENT (verb)

I ☐

Dictation. Listen to these sentences and write down the words that are missing.

1 Three .... were .... yesterday afternoon.
2 Please send a .... with your ....
3 My .... lives in ....
4 The .... press .... was held in
....
5 .... , you forgot to ....

Summary

The main signals for stress are:

1 Pitch change
2 Syllable length
3 Vowel quality

Check your progress

Record these words and phrases and make sure you stress the
prominent syllables (i.e. those in capitals).

1 aBOUT aSLEEP DRAma WOman WOmen phoTOgraphy
2 We were in COpenHAgen on SAturday NoVEmber the fifTEENTH.
3 I went to MaNIla in the SUMmer.
4 The CIty of WARsaw is REALly BEAUtiful.

3   Review

In the previous two units you have learned about:

Syllable structure

You should now know enough about syllable structure to:
a) recognise and produce the number of syllables in words and
    phrases accurately.
b) Know when to pronounce final 'es' and 'ed' as separate syllables.
c) Know that sometimes syllables 'disappear' in natural speech.

Stress

You should now know why and how to use stress in English:
a) Why – it helps emphasise important parts of a message.
b) How – by using the three main signals:
    i)   Pitch change
    ii) Syllable length
    iii) Vowel quality

Now try these review exercises.

A   Syllables

1 Listen and then say these words. On which words are the final 'es'
  or 'ed' pronounced as an extra syllable?

added	measures
checked	mixed
mixes	changes
managed	advantages
loves	developed

2 Listen to these words and phrases. Write down the number of
  syllables you hear.
  Example: easily   ....3......

1 excuse me	3 chocolate ....
2 above	4 expenses ....

16

5 comfortable   ....   7 perhaps   ....
6 along the road   ....   8 it's on Tuesday   ....

B   Pitch change ⌶

Listen to these common exclamations. Underline the syllable which
has the highest pitch.
Example: <u>won</u>derful

fantastic   really
super   amazing
incredible   marvellous

C   Syllable length ⌶

Listen and then identify the longest syllable in each word.
Example: today

review   basis   September
around   rocket   on Thursday
arrive   answer   the last one
degree   tourist   it's lovely

D   Vowel quality ⌶

Listen and then practise contrasting the strong and weak vowels in
these words.

one strong vowel   *two strong vowels*
camera   shampoo
wallet   cigarette
mirror   calculator
    tobacco

Check your progress

1 Record the words in Section D.
   Did you stress the correct syllable? Was there a definite contrast
   between strong and weak vowels? Were the stressed vowels
   lengthened?

2 [⸬] Listen to the recorded extract of natural speech. Write down
what you hear.
Speaker A: ....
Speaker B: ....
How many syllables did you hear in each of the speakers'
phrases?

Summary

Stressed syllable signals	Atom	aTomic
1 *Pitch change*	^{a}tom	a^{to}mic
2 *Syllable length*	a̅tȯm	a̅tomi̅c
3 *Vowel quality*	atom	atomic
a) ALL STRESSED VOWELS ARE STRONG.		tó thé STATIón
b) Most unstressed vowels are weak.		regÍsTRATIón

4 Word stress

When you hear a new word, the first thing you should notice is the stress.

Listen to these words ⌐··¬ :

extremely   reliable   machines

Underline the most stressed syllable in each word.

In English, word stress helps the listener to recognise words. Placing the stress on the wrong syllable is a common cause of misunderstanding. It is not easy to know which syllable or syllables to stress in words but there are some general 'rules' which can help you.

A ⌐··¬

Listen to the following two-syllable nouns and underline the syllable which is most strongly stressed.

1 Richard   Burton
  Humphrey   Bogart
  Margaret   Thatcher
  Ronald   Reagan

2 money   reason   permit
  product present   machine
  village window   water

What is the general pattern in two-syllable nouns? Did you find the 'odd one out' in Exercise 2?

The majority of two-syllable words are stressed on the first syllable. If you count only nouns and adjectives (no verbs), the figure is 90%.

B

Listen and then repeat these words (they are all nouns).

ENGlish   staTIStics   inforMAtion
SCIence   comPUter   regisTRAtion
PHYsics   reACtion
LANguage   linGUIstics

Can you see a pattern?

C

Listen and mark the stress placement in these words.

calculation   decision   reaction
solution   distribution   television
relation   association   operation

What is the pattern? Can you define a 'rule'?

D

Listen and mark the strongest stress placement in these words.

biology   biological   policy   political
geography   geographical   university   managerial
photography   photographical   society   sociological
technology   technological   electricity   electrical

What is the pattern? Can you define a 'rule'?

E

Listen and mark the stress placement in these words.

economic   terrific
strategic   logic
pathogenic   domestic
metabolic   statistic

F

Words often have a different stress pattern when they have a different grammatical function. Therefore, the pattern is a grammatical signal for the listener. Listen and practise these words.

Verb	*Noun*
inFORM	inforMAtion
SPEcialise	specialisAtion
exPORT	EXport

Now complete the columns below and underline the most stressed syllable.

Verb	*Noun*
present	....
examine	....
....	production
reduce	....
....	record
insult	....

Noun	*Adjective*
history	....
....	secretarial
analysis	....
....	political

G

Underline the most strongly stressed syllable in these words. Then listen and practise saying them.

personality	antibiotic
computerisation	surgical
pharmacology	digital
analytical	microscopic
agricultural	transmission

Check your progress

1 Record yourself saying these sentences. Check that you have the correct stress pattern in words with more than one syllable.

   a) There will be a lot of technological advances in the next five years.
   b) He's the chairman of the Industrial Development Association.
   c) New production techniques have led to significant reductions in cost.

2 Look at the lists of words below and underline the most stressed syllables. Try and find a 'rule' to explain each pattern.

   a) Reagan   Thatcher   science   city   Taylor   entrance language
   b) dramatic   atomic   allergic   static   elastic
   c) television   occasion   profession   celebration   revision solution
   d) industrial   geography   political   economy   occasional economical   security

3 Listen to this extract of natural speech. Mark the syllables you hear stressed.

   '... it's an English Language Training Consultancy ... specialising in industry-specific language training.'

Summary

Word stress rules

1 *Stress on first syllable*
Most two-syllable nouns and adjectives have stress on the first syllable:
e.g. BUTter   PRETty

2 *Stress on last syllable*
Most two-syllable verbs have stress on the last syllable:
e.g. beGIN   proDUCE

3 *Stress on penultimate syllable* (second from the end)
Words ending in 'ic':
e.g. STATic   reaLIStic
Words ending in 'sion' and 'tion':
e.g. teleVISion   soLUtion

4 *Stress on anti-penultimate syllable* (third from the end)
Words ending in 'cy', 'ty', 'phy', 'gy':
e.g. deMOCracy   reliaBILity
Words ending in 'al':
e.g. CRItical   ecoNOMical

5 *'Polysyllabic' words* (words with many syllables)
These usually have more than one stress, i.e. a 'primary' and 'secondary' stress:
e.g. interNATional   antibiotic
Often such words contain a prefix (as with 'inter' and 'anti' above) and this prefix has a secondary stress (this is common with many long technical words).

6 *'Compound' words* (words with two parts)
If the compound is a noun, the stress goes on the first part:
e.g. GREENhouse   BLACKbird
If the compound is an adjective, the stress goes on the second part:
e.g. bad-TEMpered   old-FASHioned
If the compound is a verb, the stress goes on the second part:
e.g. underSTAND   overLOOK

---

5 Rhythm

Each language has its own rhythm. The rhythm of English speech depends on the alternation of stressed and unstressed syllables: this speech rhythm is important for understanding.

The most important feature of English rhythm is that syllables are not equal in duration. (Remember syllable length in Unit 2.)

Stressed syllables are long. Unstressed syllables are usually short.
Examples:

above   return   select

A long syllable is usually surrounded by shorter syllables.
Examples:

Peter   banana   Trafalgar
an apple   in London
absolute   Have some fruit   impossible   it's possible

Listen and then practise saying these words and phrases.

Trafalgar Square
Richmond Road
Oxford Circus
Hurry up
Are you ready?
Just a minute

24

When two or more stressed syllables come together, length is added to each syllable: this makes the speech sound stronger. Listen and then practise saying these sentences.

Get out!   Birds don't eat grass.
Please come here.   Put that down now!
Don't talk nonsense.   Bring hot water.

A

You will hear twelve sentences. Do you hear a series of stressed syllables or is the sentence made of syllables of different lengths? Make two columns under the following headings, with the numbers 1 to 12. As you listen, put a cross in the appropriate column.

Regular syllable length   *Irregular syllable length*
(all stressed syllables)   (stressed and unstressed syllables)

B

The last three words in this sentence are dramatically slowed down because there are three long syllables together. Listen and repeat.

— — —
go right now
if you go right now
in time
get there in time
you might get there in time
You might get there in time if you go right now.

Now listen and repeat the following sentences making sure you stress the last three syllables in the same way.

1 The government intends to stop all strikes.
2 The robbers were finally arrested today after a ten-week search.

>>>→

C

Listen to this limerick and then practise the rhythm.

> There WAS an old MAN with a BEARD,
> Who SAID, 'It is JUST as I FEARED! –
>   Two OWLS and a HEN,
>   Four LARKS and a WREN,
> Have ALL built their NESTS in my BEARD!'

(Edward Lear)

D

A word said by itself is like a small phrase; it must have all the rhythm and stress of a phrase.

Match the rhythm of the phrases in the right-hand column with the rhythm of the words in the left-hand column.

Example:

simplification   ⟷   such a reduction

computerisation	the action
interruption	he works at the station
addition	another option
clarification	shocked the nation
communication	who did she mention

Now listen and practise saying the words and phrases in the correct order.

E

Read this poem with a partner, or in two groups.

Late

A

Are you ready?
Are you ready?

Hurry up!
Hurry up!

Come on, Allan,
Hurry up!

Hurry up.

Hurry up!

We'll be late.
We'll be late.

We'll be late.

At last.
At last!

B

Not quite. Just a minute.

Don't rush me.
Don't rush me.

I'm coming.

I'm coming.
I'm coming.

All right!

No, we won't. Don't panic.

No, we won't.
No, we won't.

Here I am.

What's the rush?

Check your progress 🔲

Listen to the recorded extract of natural speech, and write down exactly what you hear.

6 Basic sentence stress

English rhythm is based not only on word stress (i.e. the stress on a certain syllable or syllables in a word) but also on sentence stress (i.e. the basic emphasis pattern of a sentence). Both of these elements are important for intelligibility.

In most sentences there are two types of words: *content* words and *structure* words. Content words normally carry the most information. Look at this telegram message:

SEND MONEY BOUGHT BIKE

This is not a complete sentence, but the words carry the important information; they are all content words. Content words are usually emphasised. We can expand the message:

SEND me MONEY I've BOUGHT a BIKE

And further:

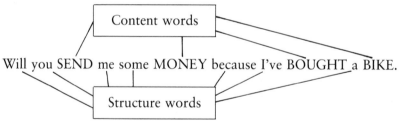

Structure words do not carry so much information. They are not normally emphasised.

What sort of words are content words, and what sort of words are structure words? Try and make a list.

Content words	e.g. nouns
Structure words	e.g. articles

A ⌨

A word is emphasised when it contains a stressed syllable. Listen and then practise these examples.

1 I WANT a baNAna.
2 The proFESSor is FAmous.
3 The BUS is COming.

4 She's WRItten the rePORT.
5 It's DIFficult to underSTAND.
6 He's PLANning to reTIRE.

B ⌨

Listen and then underline the content words in the following sentences.

1 Can I have a coffee and a cup of tea, please?
2 Would you like another one?
3 Thanks for a lovely meal.
4 Sorry but I can't come on Monday because I'm working late.
5 I've never been to a car rally.
6 I usually visit my parents on Tuesdays.

C

Look at these telex messages and see if you can expand them into complete sentences.
Example: SEND PARCEL AIRMAIL.
             'Could you send the parcel by airmail?'

(There is more than one possible version in most cases.)
1 CONFIRM ARRIVAL ORDER NO 235/SA.
2 PLEASE CONTACT. URGENT MESSAGE.
3 REGRET DELAY DUE FERRY STRIKE.
4 ARRIVING MILAN AIRPORT TUES 09.00.
5 CONFERENCE POSTPONED. CANCEL FLIGHTS.

D ⌨

Listen to these telephone messages for Chris from his boss. Then write down the messages as notes on the message pad on page 30. Write only the essential information, i.e. content words. The first one has been done for you.

TELEPHONE MESSAGE

From: Jane Croft

To: ....

MESSAGES

1 Contact Mrs Williams before 5. Urgent.

2 ....

3 ....

4 ....

Check your progress

1 Read the following dialogue. Underline the content words. Then record yourself saying this dialogue several times.

A: What's the matter?
B: I've lost my keys.
A: Where did you put them?
B: If I knew, I could find them!

2 ⌣ Listen to the recorded extract of natural speech and write down exactly what you hear.

Summary

Basic sentence stress				
Content words (stressed)				
nouns	**main verbs**	**negative auxiliaries**	**adverbs**	**adjectives**
(bike)	(send)	(don't, can't)	(quickly)	(big)
Structure words (not stressed)				
pronouns	**prepositions**	**articles**	**'to be' verbs**	
(he, she)	(on, at)	(a, the)	(is, was)	
conjunctions	**auxiliary verbs**			
(and, but)	(can, do, will)			

7 Reductions and contractions

As speech becomes more rapid or informal, it becomes more difficult to distinguish individual words. Certain changes occur in unstressed words (structure words) because of rhythm. Vowels are reduced in length and some sounds can contract or even disappear completely. If you know that you should expect changes it will help you when listening to natural, rapid speech.

Reductions

Reduction is a fundamental characteristic of English and helps explain why written English is so different from spoken English.

Structure words (see Summary in previous unit), can often be pronounced in two different ways: in their *strong* form or in their *weak*, reduced form. It is important to know when these forms can and cannot be used. In ordinary, rapid speech such words occur much more frequently in their weak form than in their strong form. Look at this example:

a) 'Look át this.'
b) 'What are you looking at?'

In (a) the vowel in 'at' is in its *weak* or reduced form, but in (b) the vowel is *strong*.

Strong form rules

These structure words usually have full vowels when they are:
i)   at the end of a sentence
ii) used for emphasis
iii) used for contrast

A 🔲

Listen and then practise these dialogues. Make sure you use the strong and weak forms correctly.

1 **Emphasis on 'do' and 'that'**
   A: Which one dó you want? This one?
   B: No.
   A: Well, which one **do** you want?
   B: **That** one.
   A: Which one?
   B: The one thát I'm pointing to.

2 **'To' at the end of a sentence**
   A: Why don't you try tó stop?
   B: I've tried **to**.

3 **Contrasting 'you'**
   A: I'm surprised yóu find it so difficult.
   B: Well, how did **you** stop?

B 🔲

When structure words begin with 'h', e.g. 'her', 'his', 'him', etc., the initial 'h' often disappears when the word is in its weak form. *Example:* Leave ĥim alone.

Listen to these sentences. Which version do you hear, (a) or (b)? Practise saying them.

1 a) Did (h)e go?
   b) Did he go?
2 a) Is (h)e here?
   b) Is she here?
3 a) Leave (h)im alone.
   b) Leave (h)er alone.

4 a) Give (h)im the pen.
   b) Give me the pen.
5 a) Is (h)er work good?
   b) Is our work good?

C 🔲

Note: The letter 'h' is not omitted when the pronoun is especially emphasised or comes at the beginning of a sentence. In these cases the pronoun must be very clear.
   Listen and practise saying this dialogue.
A: Her ideas are brilliant.
B: His project is excellent.
A: She works hard.

B: **He** works hard too.
A: **He's** good but **she's** better. (*contrast*)
B: I want **him**! (*special emphasis or contrast*)
A: I want **her**!

D

Listen to the dialogue.

A: When did (h)e go there?
B: I don't know.
A: Who did (h)e talk to?
B: I don't know.
A: Have you talked to (h)im yet?
B: Yes, I have.
A: Did you ask (h)im?
B: What?
A: Did you ask (h)im who (h)e was with?
B: Yes, I did.
A: What did (h)e say?
B: He said it's none of your business.

Now practise taking A's part.

Contractions

It is important to know that when native speakers of English talk naturally, quite a lot of sounds that you might expect to hear are not actually pronounced. Here are some examples:

Verb forms

Where've (have) you been?   I'd've (would have) come if I'd (had)
I'll (will) do it.   known.

Some verb forms can also be contracted in natural, rapid speech.
These are usually auxiliary verbs.
Example: The verb 'have' has different uses:
main verb: I have a watch.
auxiliary: I have bought a watch. (I've bought)
                 I have got a watch.* (I've got)
modal: I have to buy a watch.

* With the verb 'have got', 'have' is an auxiliary and therefore can
be contracted.

E

In the sentences below, draw a line through the letters which can be omitted in the verb 'have'.
Example: How long ~~h~~ave you been here?

1 I have got a cold.
2 Do you think he has gone?
3 Where have they been?
4 I have to do some shopping.
5 We have got to work hard.
6 She has three children.
7 Have you seen John?
8 I have never been to Japan.

Other auxiliary verbs (e.g. is, will, can) are also contracted in spoken language and in informal writing (but not in formal writing). Contractions are used to de-emphasise the less important words. This helps to highlight the more important words.

Formal	*Informal*	*Formal*	*Informal*
I am	I'm	I would/should	I'd
we are	we're	I will	I'll
you are	you're	I will not	I won't
he is	he's	I do not	I don't
that is	that's	I cannot	I can't
there is	there's		

F ⌣

Dictation. See if you can complete this telephone conversation. Write the words exactly as they are spoken. Underline the contractions.

A: Hello, George. This is Sylvia. Can I speak to Jane?
B: Oh hello, Sylvia. Yes, of course. .... with
.... in a minute. .... just come in
.... taking .... coat off. By the way,
John and Barbara called .... said ....
going .... Portugal next week. .... said
.... tell you .... calling
.... see .... all right ....
operation.

G

Negative auxiliaries are also usually contracted in spoken English, but they are stressed to emphasise the idea of 'negation'.

Formal	*Informal*
they are not coming	they aren't coming
	they're not coming
he has not gone	he hasn't gone
	he's not gone
we will not be there	we won't be there
	we'll not be there
I would not tell him	I wouldn't tell him
	I'd not tell him

Listen to the recorded dialogues and write down B's responses exactly as you hear them.

1 A: Haven't you finished that report yet?
   B: ....
2 A: I didn't see Steve yesterday.
   B: ....
3 A: Do you think Susan has left already?
   B: ....
4 A: I'm afraid we won't be able to make it this evening.
   B: ....

H

When an auxiliary verb comes at the end of a sentence, it cannot be contracted, because the word was placed there for special emphasis.

Underline the auxiliary verbs that should be contracted and then practise saying these sentences.

1 No, I do not think she has.
2 I am tired. I think I will go to bed.
3 Maybe they will.
4 He is sure you are.
5 They would help you if they could.
6 No, I should not imagine he is.

I

Dictation. Listen to Ms Wright's secretary reading back a letter which Ms Wright has dictated to her. After each 'bleep', pause the tape and write down what the secretary says. Write it as a letter (i.e. in formal style) with the full forms of the verbs. *Example:*

Spoken message　　　　　*Written message*
'I'd love to come ...'　　　'I would love to come ...'

Start the letter like this: 'Dear Mr Norlin,'

When you have finished, listen to the complete letter.

J

Disappearing syllables. Do you remember 'Disappearing syllables' in Unit 1? Sometimes weak vowels in unstressed syllables disappear, giving the impression that the syllable is missing.
Example: chocolate　　　choc(o)late

Now listen and mark the sounds that disappear in these words.

1 police
2 secretary
3 perhaps
4 vegetable
5 excuse me
6 correct
7 potato
8 comfortable
9 I'm afraid so
10 because

K

Consonant clusters. Consonants can also weaken or disappear, to avoid complex groups of consonants.
Example: acts　　　ac(t)s
　　　　　scripts　　scrip(t)s

Now listen and mark the consonants that disappear.

1 textbooks
2 next week
3 three-fifths
4 he must be ill
5 he asked Paul
6 she looked back quickly

Check your progress

1 Record the letter you wrote in Exercise I as if you were reading it to someone in informal, spoken style. Check for the presence or absence of the 'h' sound, and all contractions.

2 ⌣ Listen to the recorded extract of natural speech and complete the dialogue.

A: How .... keeping since I last saw you?
B: Not so bad. ...., actually. .... to Sweden for a couple of weeks . . .
A: And .... no problems since I last saw you?
B: None at all. No, ... OK.

Summary

Common reductions and contractions

1 Structure words usually have two forms, i.e. 'weak' and 'strong'. Weak forms are used when the word is not stressed, i.e.
   i)   at the end of a sentence
   ii) used for emphasis
   iii) used for contrast

2 When weak forms begin with 'h', the initial 'h' often disappears, e.g. Give (h)er it.

3 Auxiliary verbs can be contracted in natural rapid speech, if unstressed.

4 A syllable containing an unstressed, reduced vowel, i.e. /e/, is often deleted, e.g. p(er)haps, diff(e)rent.

5 Consonants can change or disappear in complex groups of consonants, i.e.:
   't' and 'd': often disappear between two other consonants, e.g. ac(t)s, soun(d)s; they often weaken (or are replaced by a glottal stop) before 'p' or 'b', e.g. tha(t) book, goo(d) point.

   'n': often sounds like 'm' before 'p' and 'b', e.g. he ca(m) pay, o(m) purpose.

---

8 Linking

⊡ Listen to the recorded sentences. How many words do you hear in each one?

a) ....

b) ....

In the last unit we looked at some of the changes that occur when speech becomes rapid and informal (i.e. how unstressed words can be reduced or contracted). Another element of natural speech is that words are not spoken separately but are linked together.

There are two sorts of linking:

1 Words ending in a consonant sound are linked to words beginning in a vowel sound.
   Example: sit up   read it   turn off   is (h)e

2 Words ending in a vowel sound are linked to words beginning in a vowel sound.
   Example: you are   I always   we ought

Consonant–to–vowel

When a word ends in a consonant, that final sound is often moved to the beginning of the next word, e.g. 'turn it off' = 'tur ni toff'.

A ⊡

Listen to these words and then practise saying them.

will I   laugh at
where I   with us
when I   push over
come on   miss (h)im
give up   sing it

Note: Silent 'h' words, starting with an 'h' which can be omitted, are treated as if they begin with a vowel, e.g.
'Is (h)e busy' sounds like 'izzybizzy'.
'Give (h)er it' sounds like 'giverit'.
'What's (h)is name' sounds like 'watsiz name'.

B ⌣

Listen to this dialogue. Mark the links.
Example: Can I help you?

A: Can I help you, sir?
B: Yes, I'm in a rush I'm afraid. Can I have a piece of apple cake
    please, with ice cream?
A: Certainly, sir. I'll ask the waiter to come over as soon as
    possible.

Now listen and repeat these phrases.

I'm afraid
I'm in a rush
I'm in a rush I'm afraid.

piece of apple
a piece of apple cake
Can I
Can I have a
Can I have a piece of apple cake, please?

soon as
as soon as possible
come over
to come over as soon as possible
I'll ask
I'll ask the waiter to come over as soon as possible.

Now practise the dialogue either in pairs or with the cassette, taking
turns to be A or B.

C ⌣

Listen to these words and then practise saying them.

keep it	thank us
cube of	hang it
sit on	large egg
said it	switch off

D

Listen to this dialogue. Mark the links.
Example: Switch off the light.

A: Switch off the light, David. It's almost eleven.
B: I'm scared of the dark. I think I heard a noise. Look over there!
   Something on the window ledge is moving!

Now listen and repeat these phrases.

David
the light, David
Switch off
Switch off the light, David.
almost eleven
It's almost eleven.

scared of
scared of the dark

heard a
I heard a noise
think I
I think I heard a noise.

ledge is
the window ledge is
Something on
Something on the window ledge is moving!

Now practise the dialogue in pairs or with the cassette, taking turns
to be A or B.

Vowel–to–vowel

E 😐

Listen and then practise saying these linked words.

do[w]I   no[w]other
who[w]are   too[w]often
know[w]if   though[w]I
how[w]often   you[w]ought

Listen to the dialogue. Mark the links.

A: How often do I have to do it?
B: You ought to do every exercise once a week.
A: Do I have to do *every* exercise?
B: Yes, it should take you about two hours. Though I don't suppose it will!

F 😐

Listen and then practise saying these linked words.

may[y]I   she[y]answers
she[y]is   high[y]up
we[y]ought   they[y]end

Listen to the dialogue. Mark the links.

A: Actually, I ought to practise more regularly I suppose.
B: Well, don't worry about it. I often forget myself.
A: Perhaps we ought to try and go together.

G 😐

Dictation. Listen and complete the dialogue.

A: .... , Edward?
B: .... bad .... exactly
.... place though.
A: .... staying?
B: .... pub .... edge ....
A: .... what .... doing .... ?
B: .... actually. .... evening
.... TV, ... snack ....
town .... football afterwards.

Now listen again and mark all the possible links.

Check your progress

Practise the dialogue in Exercise E with a partner or the cassette, and then record it.

Summary

Linking rules

1 Words ending in a consonant followed by words beginning in a vowel: the final consonant links to the initial vowel, e.g. this evening.

2 Words ending in a vowel followed by words beginning in a vowel: the words are linked by inserting a sort of 'w' or 'y' sound, e.g.
'w' sound – if the vowel at the end of the first word is rounded (i.e. has a rounded lip position).
'y' sound – if the vowel at the end of the first word is spread (i.e. has a spread or stretched lip position), e.g. so(w) I'll, I(y) am.

3 Words ending in 'r' followed by words beginning with a vowel: the final 'r' (although not pronounced in isolation in standard southern English) is linked to the next word, e.g. where is, are in.

9 Review

In the previous units you have learned:
1 How to use stress and rhythm in words and phrases.
2 How stress and rhythm affect speech, resulting in contracted
 syllables, reduced vowels and linking between words.

Now try these review exercises.

A Stress patterns

Group these words into two columns according to their stress
pattern.

Example:
Column 1   *Column 2*
RElative   absoLUtely

relative	agency	economic	managerial
participate	absolutely	technological	solution
photograph	argumentative	indication	mechanic
alternative	statistic	photographic	photography

B English rhythm 📼

A word said by itself is like a small sentence; it has stressed parts
and unstressed parts, strong vowels and weak vowels. It must have
all the rhythm and emphasis of a sentence. Listen and then practise
saying the following 'pairs'.

1 átTRACtive   ít's ACtive
2 refuGEE   have sóme TEA
3 réSPONsíble   ít's POSSíble
4 electrífíCAtíón   she went tó thé STAtíón

C Basic sentence stress ⌶

1 Listen to this dialogue and underline the content words.

> A: Are you ready?
> B: Not quite.
> A: Put your coat on.
> B: Just a minute. Don't rush me!

2 Listen to the beginning of this song by Laurie Anderson. Underline the content words and then practise saying it while you listen.

> Good evening. This is your Captain.
> We are about to attempt a crash landing.
>   Please extinguish all cigarettes.
>   Place your tray tables in their upright, locked position.
> Your Captain says: Put your head on your knees.
> Your Captain says: Put your head in your hands.

D Reductions/contractions and linking ⌶

Dictation. Listen to the recorded sentences. Write them down as you listen. There are five sentences.

10   Sentence focus 1

We have seen how native speakers of English use a basic stress
pattern in speech, i.e. content words are usually stressed and structure words are usually unstressed.

However, speakers can choose which information they want to
highlight. We can focus the listener's attention on the parts of the
message that are most important in a particular context.

1 When a conversation begins, the focus is usually on the last
content word.
Examples: What's the <u>matter</u>?
Where are you <u>going</u>?
Put the <u>coffee</u> in it.

2 The focus of a sentence can be broad.
Examples: I've <u>lost</u> my <u>keys</u>.
My flight leaves at <u>11.30</u> on <u>Tuesday</u> the <u>sixth</u>.
He's <u>stolen</u> my <u>bag</u>.
(The focus is on more than one word, or a phrase, but the centre
of focus is on the last content word, i.e. 'bag'.)

3 The focus can be narrow.
Examples: <u>Here</u> they are!
I'm not <u>ready</u>.
<u>Who's</u> stolen your bag?
(The focus is on one word.)

You can emphasise any word or phrase in a sentence. Focus is used
to highlight an idea or piece of information. The speaker can choose
to focus the listener's attention either on new information (i.e. something mentioned for the first time) or old information (i.e. something
mentioned or referred to before).

A ⌣

Listen to these dialogues.

1 A: I've lost my <u>hat</u>. (basic stress pattern: the content word is
                   focussed)
   B: What <u>kind</u> of hat? ('hat' is now an old idea; 'kind' is the new
                   focus)
   A: It was a <u>sun</u> hat.
   B: What <u>colour</u> sun hat?
   A: It was <u>white</u>. White with <u>stripes</u>.
   B: There was a white hat with stripes in the <u>car</u>.
   A: <u>Which</u> car?
   B: The one I <u>sold</u>.

2 A: I want some <u>shoes</u>.
   B: What <u>kind</u> of shoes?
   A: <u>Suede</u> shoes.
   B: <u>Black</u> or <u>brown</u>?
   A: <u>Neither</u>. I want <u>blue</u> shoes. With <u>thick black soles</u>!

B ⌣

Listen and practise saying these dialogues, using the same focus
pattern.

1 A: Where are you going?
   B: America.
   A: Where in America? To the east or to the west?
   B: Neither. I've already been east and west. I'm going south.

2 A: Are you going on holiday?
   B: No. I'm going to study.
   A: Study what? Maths or English?
   B: Neither. I'm sick of maths and English. I'm going to study
      engineering. Electronic engineering.

C

Practise saying the following dialogue. Substitute your own new
information (focus) for the words in parentheses.

   A: Are you from (<u>England</u>)?
   B: No, I'm from (<u>Argentina</u>).
   A: How long have you <u>been</u> here?
   B: I've been here for (<u>three months</u>).

A: What are you <u>studying</u>?
B: (<u>English</u>.)
A: Do you find (English) <u>difficult</u>?
B: (<u>Yes</u>, a <u>little</u>.)

D

Underline the focus words and then listen and practise the dialogue.

A: Hello. What's new?
B: Nothing much. What's new with you?
A: I'm going to the States.
B: East coast or West coast?
A: West. I want to visit San Francisco.

E

Underline the focus words in the dialogue below and then practise
it. (Different people may emphasise different words.)

A: Do you think British food is expensive?
B: Not really.
A: Well, I think it's expensive.
B: That's because you eat in restaurants.
A: Where do you eat?
B: At home.
A: I didn't know you could cook?
B: Well, actually, I can't. I just eat bread and cheese.
A: That's awful!
B: No, it isn't. I like bread and cheese.
A: You're crazy!

Check your progress

1 Record the dialogue in Exercise E. Did you emphasise the focus
  words? Did you definitely not emphasise the 'old' information?
  The contrast between emphasis and lack of emphasis is very
  important.

2 ☐ Listen to the recorded extract of natural speech. Write down
  exactly what you hear and then mark the focus words.

11 Sentence focus 2

Sentence focus helps the speaker emphasise the most significant information in his or her message. The speaker can choose which word or words to focus to contrast information.

Let's look at some common uses of contrastive focus.

1 To correct information:
   Example: A: Why didn't you phone <u>Jim</u>?
             B: But I <u>did</u> phone him!
             A: Have you ever visited <u>Rome</u>?
             B: No, <u>I</u> haven't, but my <u>sister</u> has.

2 To check information:
   Example: A: I didn't <u>go</u> after all.
             B: You didn't <u>go</u>?

Correcting information

We can focus words to contradict or deny any idea in a previous sentence. This pattern is common when we want to correct information.

⌷ *Example:* A: Here you are. <u>Two teas</u> and a <u>coffee</u>.
          B: But we didn't want <u>two</u> teas. We wanted <u>one</u>.

A ⌷

Listen to this dialogue and then practise it. Make sure you emphasise the focus words.

A: Good <u>morning</u>. May I <u>help</u> you?
B: Yes, I'd like to speak to Mr <u>Williams</u>, please.
A: What's your <u>name</u>, please?
B: John <u>Ribble</u>.
A: Mr <u>Williams</u>. There's a Mr <u>Riddle</u> to see you.
B: Excuse me, not <u>Riddle</u>, <u>Ribble</u>.
A: Oh, sorry. There's a Mr <u>Ribble</u> to see you, Mr Williams.

B 📟

Read the dialogue and see if you can mark the focus words. The first two lines have been marked for you.

Customer: Can I have <u>one cheese sandwich</u> and <u>two ham rolls</u>, please?
Waiter: That's <u>one</u> ham sandwich ...
Customer: No, one cheese sandwich.
Waiter: Sorry, that's one cheese sandwich and two ham sandwiches.
Customer: No, two ham rolls.
Waiter: Right ... You did want two cheese sandwiches, didn't you?
Customer: No, I didn't. Just one.
Waiter: Oh. I think I'd better write this down.

Now listen to the dialogue and check the focus.

Notice how the focus in a question shows what the person wants to know. The answer we give depends on the word which had the most emphasis in the question.
Example: Waiter: You did want <u>two</u> cheese sandwiches, didn't you?
Customer: No, I <u>didn't</u>. Just <u>one</u>.

C

We can focus words to indicate some information which is in contrast to a preceding sentence.
Example: A: The train leaves at a quarter to four.
B: No, it's a quarter <u>past</u> four.

Now look at the questions below and underline the word in the responses which is in focus.

1 A: <u>Were</u> you in the bank on Friday?
B: No, I wasn't.
2 A: Were <u>you</u> in the bank on Friday?
B: No, but my sister was.
3 A: Were you <u>in</u> the bank on Friday?
B: No, but I was near it.
4 A: Were you in the <u>bank</u> on Friday?
B: No, but I was in the post office, next door.
5 A: Were you in the bank on <u>Friday</u>?
B: No, but I was there on Thursday.

Now practise reading the dialogue in pairs.

49

D ⌣

Listen to the policeman asking a woman about a bank robbery. Notice which word he focusses on in each sentence. After each 'bleep' choose the appropriate reply and put a cross by it.
Example:
1 Policeman: Excuse me, madam, but were <u>you</u> in the bank on
            Friday?
  Reply: a) No, but my <u>sister</u> was. ....✗.......
         b) No, but I was <u>near</u> it.   ....

Now continue:
2 Reply: a) No, on <u>Thursday</u>. ....
        b) Yes, <u>every</u> Friday. ....
3 Reply: a) No, but I <u>heard</u> them.   ....
        b) No, I just saw the <u>guards</u>. ....
4 Reply: a) No, I <u>screamed</u>.   ....
        b) No, someone <u>else</u> did. ....
5 Reply: a) No, I think there were <u>two</u>.   ....
        b) No, I think there was a <u>woman</u>. ....

Checking information

We can focus words to query a previous speaker's sentence.
⌣ *Example:* A: It took me <u>two hours</u> to get to work this
           morning.
        B: Two <u>hours</u>?

E ⌣

Now try and give a suitable response to query each of the sentences you hear.

F ⌣

Shifting the focus can affect the listener's interpretation of the message, so it is important to recognise the most emphasised word.
Example: I thought it was going to <u>rain</u>. (but it didn't)
       I <u>thought</u> it was going to rain. (and it did)

Listen to the conversation between Paul and Barbara. Is Barbara confirming what actually happened or querying something? Put a cross in the appropriate column.

	Confirming	*Querying*
Example:		
1 I thought you'd have a nice time.	......×.......	....
2 I thought you were going to Spain.	....	....
3 But I thought you were going with Maria.	....	....
4 I rather thought there might be problems.	....	....
5 I thought you'd been there.	....	....
6 I thought you spoke Italian.	....	....
7 I thought you were coming to my party on Saturday.	....	....

Check your progress ⊡

Underline the focus in B's answers below. Then listen to the dialogues and repeat B's part.

1 A: Oh, I'll have to go and get the paper.
   B: I'll get it for you.
2 A: When can I collect the photographs?
   B: I'm afraid they won't be ready until Tuesday.
3 A: I'm glad you're coming on Friday.
   B: But I can't come.
4 A: Can you finish that by five o'clock?
   B: But I've already finished it.
5 A: What did you think of the film?
   B: Well, I thought it was rather boring.

12   Review

Summary

In the last two units we looked at how to call the listener's attention to what is important.

Sentence emphasis	
Basic sentence stress	**Content** words are usually stressed. **Structure** words are usually not stressed. e.g. We WANT an ELECtion.
Focus	The **final content** word in a sentence is usually the **focus**. e.g. He wants some <u>shoes</u>.
New focus	We can focus on any word or words that give **new information** in a conversation. e.g. A: What <u>kind</u> of shoes? B: The <u>flat</u> kind.
Contrastive focus	We can emphasise focus words to **contrast** an idea with a previous idea, e.g. when **correcting** or **checking** information.

A   Basic sentence stress ⌕

Listen to these sentences and underline the content words.

1 The Queen is visiting Sydney this morning.
2 Do you want a cup of tea?
3 Can you tell him I called?
4 I'm sorry to trouble you but it's rather urgent.

B Focus 😑

Listen to these sentences and underline the focus words.

1 The film was fantastic!
2 Are you coming to the party on Saturday?
3 Can you give it to him?
4 I think I left it in the bedroom.

C New focus 😑

Listen to the following conversation and underline the focus words.
Notice the changes in focus.

A: What are you doing?
B: I came to see Peter.
A: Well, Peter's not here.
B: I can see he's not here. Where is he?
A: I don't know where he is.
B: Not very friendly, are you?
A: Neither are you!

D Contrastive focus 😑

Listen to the dialogues and underline the focus words.

1 A: Peter is funny.
  B: He isn't funny. He's strange.
2 A: So the number is 35487.
  B: No, it's 35187.
3 A: That's £3.15 altogether.
  B: £3.50?
  A: No, £3.15.

13   Thought groups 1

In the last few units we have seen how speakers can use elements
such as rhythm, stress and focus to help listeners understand
messages. Now we will look at other important speech signals, i.e.
pause and pitch movement (intonation).

   When we speak, we need to divide speech up into small 'chunks'
to help the listener understand messages. These chunks or thought
groups are groups of words which go together to express one idea or
thought. In English, we use pauses and low pitch to mark the end of
thought groups.

A ☺

When you read numbers aloud over the telephone (addresses,
telephone numbers, etc.) it is important to group the words correctly.

   Listen to the following series of numbers. Then practise pauses to
mark the end of each group.

1 a) 5282   0149
  b) 52   82   01   49
2 a) 95   616
  b) 95   61   6
3 a) 916   756   5183
  b) 916   7565   183

Ask a partner or the rest of the class to guess if you read (a) or (b).

B ☺

Listen and then practise saying the following sentences, using pauses
to mark the end of a group.

1 Can you tell him,   if you see him?
2 I read a really good book,   when I was on holiday.
3 We went to the cinema,   and then we had a drink.
4 I quite like rice,   but I prefer potatoes.
5 It was very cold last winter,   especially around Christmas.

C ▱

Listen to the following equations. Then practise saying them, using pauses and low pitch to show the end of each group.

1 $(A + B) \times C = Y$ (A plus B,   multiplied by C,   equals Y)
2 $A + (B \times C) = D$ (A,   plus B multiplied by C,   equals D)
3 $A - (B \times C) = Y$
4 $(A - B) \times C = Y$
5 $(X \div Y) - A = B$

D ▱

Listen to the recorded mathematical calculations. Write down the answers. The correct answer depends on correct grouping.

E ▱

It is important to group words together clearly so that the listener gets the right message.

Listen and then practise saying this dialogue. Make sure you group the right couples together!

A: Who's coming tonight?
B: John.
A: Just John?
B: No, John and Susie.
A: No one else?
B: Well, there's Bob.
A: Alone?
B: No, with Anne.
A: So, that's John and Susie and Bob and Anne. Is that it?
B: Oh, and Gordon. On his own.
A: So that's John and Susie and Bob and Anne and Gordon.
B: Yes, that's right.

F 🔲

Two sentences written the same way may have a different meaning.
Marking the thought groups clearly helps distinguish the difference
in meaning.

Listen to the different emphasis in the following pairs of sentences.
Do you hear (a) or (b)? Put a cross by the one you hear.

1 a) The man and the woman dressed in black,   came out of the
      restaurant.   ....
   b) The man,   and the woman dressed in black,   came out of the
      restaurant.   ....

2 a) Alfred said, 'the boss is stupid.'   ....
   b) 'Alfred,'   said the boss,   'is stupid.'   ....

3 a) If you finish, quickly leave the room.   ....
   b) If you finish quickly,   leave the room.   ....

4 a) Holding the handle firmly,   turn the lever to the
      right.   ....
   b) Holding the handle,   firmly turn the lever to the
      right.   ....

5 a) He sold his house,   boat,   and car.   ....
   b) He sold his houseboat,   and car.   ....

G 🔲

Throw away thought groups. Sometimes a speaker adds information
or an idea which is not really essential, i.e. it can be 'thrown away'.
We can signal that this thought group is less important than other
ones by:
a) Lowering the pitch
b) Saying it more quietly

Listen and then practise saying the following sentences.

1 In Hong Kong, ↓ for some reason or other, ↓ they drive on the left.

2 John, ↓ who's the one in the blue suit, ↓ has just got married again.

3 ↓ As you probably know, ↓ I'm going to China in September.

Underline the most important thought groups in A's sentences below.

A: Alison is leaving work, so I've been told.
B: Really!
A: Don't tell anyone, but ... she's been sacked!
B: No!
A: Her husband, who's over there talking to Jean, is very upset about it.
B: Oh dear.
A: They're moving, so they say, to the south.

Now listen to the dialogue.

H ⌷

If you cannot think of a word in the middle of a thought group, do not stop! Use an English 'hesitation expression' so that you do not have to pause too long (this can suggest that it is the end of a thought group, and be confusing).

Some English hesitation expressions:
um ..., er ..., well ..., you know ..., I mean ..., you see...

Listen to the dialogue and see if you can write down what Pat says, without the hesitations.

Example:
Mother: Did you have a nice afternoon with the kids, Pat?
Pat: Oh ... er ... yes ... er ... we got on ... um ... pretty well.
         Yes, we got on pretty well.

Now continue.

Check your progress

1 Record the sentence pairs in Exercise F. Did you carefully distinguish between them?

2 ⌷
   Listen to the recorded extract of natural speech and write down the two telephone numbers. Make sure you group the numbers together correctly.

   Patrick's number: ....
   The radio station's number: ....

14   Thought groups 2

Dear Vincent,

A quick 'thank-you' for your excellent
hospitality and the time you gave up for me
last week. As always I appreciated being able
to see old friends and to look around the
factory again.

Although it wasn't possible to talk much about
training programmes on this occasion, I am
confident that we will be able to work on next
year's programme as soon as your new Training
Manager starts work on November 19th.

In written English, we can help the reader by marking thought groups using punctuation, for example, commas, full stops, capital letters and paragraphs. In spoken English, we have to use other ways to help the listener understand messages.

The most common signals are pauses and pitch change. We can use these, like punctuation, to mark the introduction, continuation and conclusion of ideas in connected speech. An idea may involve only one thought group or several related thought groups.

The basic pattern is as follows:

1 High pitch marks the beginning of a new idea.
2 High pitch (often together with a short pause) marks the continuation of an idea.
3 Low pitch and a pause mark the end of an idea.

Key
↑ high pitch
↓ low pitch
/ short pause
// longer pause

You will hear extracts from three different sorts of connected speech: a lecture, a radio news broadcast and an interview.

A 😐

Listen to this extract from a lecture on 'Thought group markers'.
Read the text at the same time and notice the high and low pitch
and the pauses:

' ↑ Today I want to tell you about some useful research / on the way
English speakers help their listeners // ↓ '

B 😐

Listen to this second extract from the same lecture. On the text below:
a) Mark the pauses.
b) Mark the most important high and low pitch points (there is no
    punctuation to help you).

'each language has special ways to mark thought groups but in
English the chief marker is intonation'

C 😐

Listen to these phrases taken from the same lecture. Decide whether
the end of each phrase is the end of an idea or not.

  Yes/No
1 ....
2 ....
3 ....

D 😐

Fluency practice. Listen and repeat:

intonation
is intonation
marker
the chief marker
the chief marker is intonation
English
but in English
but in English the chief marker is intonation

groups
thought groups
to mark thought groups
ways

special ways
has special ways to mark thought groups
each language
each language has special ways to mark thought groups

Each language has special ways to mark thought groups, but in English the chief marker is intonation.

Did you put the pauses in the correct places? Did you remember the high pitch on 'each' and the low pitch on 'intonation'?
    We can use the same signals to mark a change of topic or direction in connected speech.

E

Listen to these phrases from a radio news bulletin about the death of Olof Palme, the Swedish Prime Minister. You will hear the whole bulletin in Exercise G. Listen to the introductory comment:

'The ↑Swedish Prime Minister, Mr Olof Palme, has been assassinated.'

Did you notice the high pitch on ↑'Swedish' to mark this new topic? Listen to the concluding remark about Olof Palme made by the English Prime Minister, Mrs Margaret Thatcher:

'... "I shall miss Olof Palme very deeply," she said ↓ .'

Did you notice the final very low pitch on 'said' and then a long pause to mark the end of this topic? Listen to how the news reader introduces the next topic:

'↑ Now the other news ...'

Did you notice the high pitch on 'now'? Again, this marks a new topic. Listen again to the introductory and concluding remarks about Olof Palme and try and say them yourself at the same time.

F

Listen to these phrases taken from the same news bulletin about Olof Palme. Decide whether the end of each phrase is the end of an idea or not.

    Yes/No
1 ....
2 ....
3 ....
4 ....
5 ....

G 😑

Now listen to the whole news bulletin. How many topics are there altogether?

H 😑

As well as marking thought groups and changes in topic, pause and pitch change are also used in conversational speech to signal to other speakers when you have finished speaking and when you have not.

Listen to the recorded conversation between Chris and his boss, Diana. When Diana pauses, is she going to add something else, or has she finished what she wanted to say? If you think she will add something else, say 'Yes?' after the 'bleep'. If you think she has finished, say 'Right'.

Example:
Diana: Oh, Chris, it's about the visitors ...
Chris: Yes?
Diana: They're coming on Thursday.
Chris: Right.

Now continue.

I 😑

Listen to this extract from a conversation between a training manager from Telecom Headquarters (referred to here as THQ) and an interviewer.

a) Mark the high pitch when each of the two speakers starts speaking.
b) Mark the long pause and the low pitch when the first speaker finishes speaking.

'... and of course we're in constant touch with them by telephone yes tell me er some of the sorts of problems that you er get and that would call for a visit from THQ er well one of the problems would be where we discover that something has gone wrong...'

J 〔:·:〕

Listen to four short extracts from a different part of the same interview. In each case, decide if the speaker has said all he wants to say or not.

Yes/No

1 ....
2 ....
3 ....
4 ....

Check your progress 〔:·:〕

Listen to the last part of the news recording in Exercise G again. Try and write the last news item, about Norway, as a dictation. Check what you have written and then try and read it aloud using the same pauses and pitch changes as the news reader.

15 Pitch range

In the last two units we saw how pause and pitch change help the listener understand messages. In the next two units we will look at some more functions of intonation (pitch variation).

Speakers can use the pitch of their voice to send a variety of messages because it helps express intentions. Everyone has his or her own normal pitch range.

In ordinary speech, we usually keep within the lower part of our pitch range, but if we want to express stronger feelings, or involvement, one of the signals we can use is extra pitch height.

[cassette icon] Listen to these examples:

A: Do you like cake?

B: Yes.

A: Do you like chocolate cake?

B: Yes!

A ⊡

Listen to the conversation between Peter and Sarah. Listen
particularly to how Sarah replies. Is she enthusiastic or not very
interested? After each 'bleep', draw the appropriate mouth.
Example:

    Peter: Sarah, I'm going to a party tomorrow night, would you
           like to come?

1 Sarah: Oh.

   Peter: It's just an office party really.

2 Sarah: Oh.

Now continue:

3

4

5

6

7

8

9

B   ⌐··¬

Listen to the conversation in a travel agent's. The customer is
planning to visit London and wants some information about things
to do there. He is not particularly interested in all the suggestions.
Look at the map below and put a tick beside the places he is
interested in visiting.

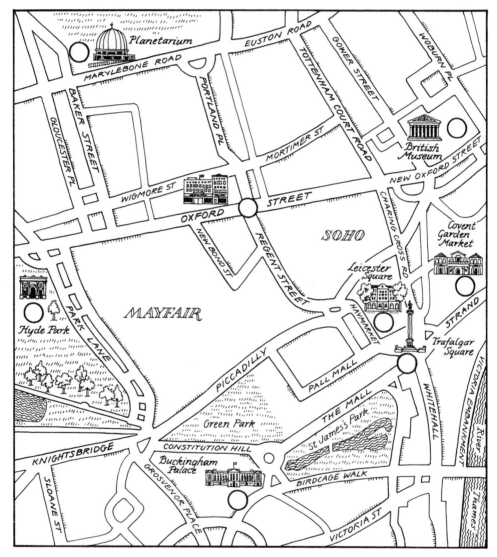

C

First listen to the conversation below, without reading it. A man and a woman are visiting someone. Their host is very welcoming. Is the man or the woman more interested and enthusiastic?

Host: I'm so glad you could come.
Man: Hello!
Woman: Hello.
Host: Do sit down.
Man: Thank you.
Woman: Thanks.
Host: Would you like a cup of tea?
Man: Mm, I'd love one.
Woman: OK.
Host: And a cake?
Man: Lovely.
Woman: Thanks.
Host: Don't you like cakes?
Woman: Not really.

Now practise the conversation either with the cassette or other students. Take turns playing the man and then the woman.

Check your progress

Record these dialogues.

1 A: Mr Smith won £50.   B: Really.
2 A: I won £50.   B: Really.
3 A: You've just won £50.   B: Really.

Did you vary the pitch range on 'Really' to show more or less interest?

16   Pitch curves

In the previous units we have looked at different aspects of intonation, i.e. pitch change and pause (signalling thought groups and the beginning and end of messages) and pitch range (signalling the speaker's involvement).

   Now we will look at another function of intonation, pitch curves, i.e. the direction or movement of pitch.

   There are two basic pitch curves:
a) Rising (showing that a message is 'open', i.e. incomplete or uncertain).
b) Falling (showing that a message is 'closed', i.e. final or certain).

▣ Listen to these examples:

A: There's no hot water.
B: There's no hot water.

What were the final pitch curves for speakers A and B?

Now let's look at some more examples, using questions. Generally, there are two main functions of questions:
1 To find out / get information (that you do not already have).
2 To check information (that you already have some idea about).

Getting information

A ▣

Listen and repeat:

Where do you live?
Where are you from?
What's your profession?

Now listen and fill in the missing words:

1 .... do you .... ?
2 .... it .... ?
3 .... do you .... it?

4 .... he .... ?
5 .... do you .... ?
6 .... she .... ?

Listen to the questions again. Was the final pitch curve rising or falling in each case?

B ⌣⌣

Before you listen to the recording, write in your part of the dialogue below.

Pat: Hello, my name's Pat. Would you like a drink?
You: ....
Pat: Are you English?
You: ....
Pat: Where exactly are you from?
You: ....
Pat: Oh, really, and have you been here very long?
You: ....
Pat: Oh, I see. Are you studying here?
You: ....
Pat: Oh, yes. Where are you staying by the way?
You: ....
Pat: Really, is it far from here?
You: ....
Pat: Mm. Well, I'm afraid I must be going. It's been nice talking to you. Bye.
You: ....

Now listen to the dialogue and take part in the conversation with Pat. Try not to refer back to the dialogue.

Listen once more and try and mark the final pitch curve (up or down) at the end of Pat's questions.

Now practise the dialogue with a partner, taking turns to be Pat. Make sure you use the same final pitch curves.

Checking information

C ⌣

1 **'Closed' messages**, i.e. checking information that you are almost certain about.

Listen and repeat:

1 You're Mexican, aren't you?
2 That's the Vatican, isn't it?
3 You don't play tennis, do you?
4 So, he doesn't really like school, does he?
5 So, you're happy here?
6 Is that the station over there?
7 Have I just to start reading now?
8 Presumably you know Linda, then?

2 **'Open' messages**, i.e. checking information that you are not very sure about.

Listen and repeat:

1 You drink coffee, don't you?
2 That's his sister, isn't it?
3 You lived in Australia for a while, is that right?
4 You locked the back door, didn't you?
5 You've skied before, haven't you?

Note: Make sure you stress the 'verb' part of a tag, e.g. 'AREN'T you?', 'DOES he?'

Asking for repetition

D ⌣

Sometimes it is necessary to repeat information if:
a) You have not heard or not understood a reply.
b) You want confirmation of a reply.

We can do this by echoing all or part of the question or the reply. Listen to these dialogues and then practise them with a partner.

Dialogue 1
A: How many people are coming?
B: Forty.

A: How many?
B: Forty.

Dialogue 2
A: How many people are coming?
B: Forty.
A: Forty?
B: Yes.

Dialogue 3
A: How many people are coming?
B: Forty.
A: Forty.
B: That's right.

Why is the final pitch curve falling in the last dialogue?

E

Listen to the dialogue and then take B's part.

A: OK. Bye then, Brian.
B: What did Brian have to say?
A: Oh, he's getting married on Friday, in Hawaii, and he's invited us to the wedding.
B: Mm ... sorry, dear, what's Brian doing?
A: He's getting married.
B: Getting married?

A: Yes, on Friday.
B: When did you say?
A: Friday.
B: Friday.
A: Yes.
B: Where's the wedding again?
A: In Hawaii.
B: Hawaii?
A: Yes. He's invited us.
B: To Hawaii?
A: Yes.
B: On Friday?
A: Yes.
B: Come on then. We'd better get a move on!

Note: Did you notice the stress on the question word when B asked A to repeat something, e.g. 'Mm ... sorry, dear. WHAT's Brian doing?'

Check your progress

1 Go back and record the questions in Exercise C. Make sure you distinguish between information you are almost sure about and information you are not very sure about.

2 ⌷ Listen to the recorded interview. Write down all the interviewer's questions. For each one, decide if it is 'checking' information or 'getting' information.

What exactly is the function of the interviewer's response 'Yes' near the beginning of the conversation?

17   Review

In the last four units we have looked at some functions of intonation (i.e. pitch variation). Intonation and sentence stress work together to help speakers send clear messages.

A   Thought groups 😐

Pauses and pitch fall mark the boundaries of thought groups.
Regular pauses and clear thought groups help listeners understand speech.
Example: 'Today // I'd like to talk to you // about new developments /'

B   Pitch range 😐

Everyone has his or her own voice range. We can use a wide range to show extra involvement, such as enthusiasm or surprise.
Example: A: I'm going to America next week.
　　　　 B: Really!

C   Pitch curves 😐

There are two basic pitch curves in English: 'falling' and 'rising'.
The speaker's final pitch curve helps the listener understand the precise meaning of a message.
Example: A: This is your bag, isn't it?
　　　　 B: No, it's Pat's.
　　　　 A: Pat's?

Check your progress 😐

Listen to the recorded extract of natural speech and, on the copy of the extract on page 74, mark:

a) The change of speaker;
b) The main pauses;

c) The pitch change (up or down) on 'systems' and 'what';
d) The pitch curve (falling or rising) on 'isn't it'.

'This is in fact one of the differences between the school systems isn't it? What about when children change from English to French and back to French...'

18 Voicing

In this section of the book, we are going to look at some essential sound contrasts in English. First we will look at consonant contrasts and then we will look at vowel contrasts.

One of the basic distinctions between English consonants is voicing. Some consonants are voiced and some are unvoiced.

Practise the difference. Press your fingers against your ears and make this sound:

sssssssssssssssssssssssssssssss (unvoiced)

Now, keeping your fingers against your ears, make this sound:

zzzzzzzzzzzzzzzzzzzzzzzzzzzzz (voiced)

Can you feel the difference? The vibration is called voicing.

Say this phrase quickly:

Is he busy?

Are the letter 's's voiced or unvoiced?

A ⌐⌐

Listen and then practise differentiating these words. Make a clear contrast.

Voiced	Unvoiced
zap	sap
phase	face
advise	advice
van	fan
service	surface
teethe	teeth
game	came
bay	pay
do	to

B

Listen to the recorded groups of words and pick out the word which sounds different in each group of four.

Example: coat   coat   <u>goat</u>   coat

C

Now listen to the recorded statements. Choose the appropriate reply to each statement. Put a cross by it.

1 Reply: a) Take it to a garage.   ....
           b) Take it to an electrician.   ....
2 Reply: a) Why? Is it hot?   ....
           b) Why? Is it broken?   ....
3 Reply: a) Well, phone her instead.   ....
           b) Well, walk if you'd rather.   ....
4 Reply: a) Yes, be careful, it's very slippery.   ....
           b) Yes, I know, they're very slow.   ....
5 Reply: a) What! It's soaking wet.   ....
           b) OK. Maybe the line is busy.   ....

D

Listen and then repeat.

buzzing noise
bees
sounds like bees
isn't it
amazing, isn't it
sound
hissing sound
snake
sort of snake

Listen to the dialogue.

A: What's that buzzing noise?
B: Sounds like bees.
A: But we're in the middle of the desert!
B: Mm. Amazing, isn't it?
A: And what's that hissing sound?
B: Sounds like a snake.
A: A snake! What sort of snake?
B: A sand snake. They're quite common here.
A: Well, that's not surprising, is it!

Now practise the dialogue with a partner.

Check your progress

Practise the dialogue in Exercise D with a partner and record it.

19 Voicing and syllable length

The difference between voiced and unvoiced final consonants is another important contrast in English. The vowel before an unvoiced final consonant is likely to be shorter. This helps the listener to identify the final consonant.

A

1 Listen to the following pairs of words and practise the contrast.

Shorter vowel	*Longer vowel*
Unvoiced final consonant	*Voiced final consonant*
safe	save
leaf	leave
ice	eyes
peace	peas
bus	buzz
back	bag
cap	cab
seat	seed
batch	badge
rich	ridge

2 Listen to the recorded groups of words and pick out the word which sounds different in each group of four.

Example: <u>feet</u> feed feed feed

B 😐

This contrast between long and short syllables and between voiced and unvoiced final consonants can also help distinguish the different grammatical function of words which are similar.

1 Listen to the following pairs of words and practise the contrast.

Voiced	*Unvoiced*
Longer syllable	*Shorter syllable*
use (verb)	use (noun)
excuse (verb)	excuse (noun)
advise (verb)	advice (noun)
prove (verb)	proof (noun)
lose (verb)	loose (adjective)
close (verb)	close (adjective)

2 Now listen and write the word you hear in the correct column. The first one is an example:

Verb	*Noun*	*Adjective*
1 ..advise....	....	....
2	....	....
3	....	....
4	....	....
5	....	....

C 😐

Listen to the recorded statements and choose the appropriate reply.
Put a cross by it.
1 Reply: a) Call a doctor.   ....
         b) Call a waiter.   ....
2 Reply: a) It's only a fly.   ....
         b) I think it's just a car.   ....
3 Reply: a) No, I'm not leaving yet.   ....
         b) No, mine is brown and checked.   ....
4 Reply: a) What! Every week? ....
         b) Did she like them?   ....

D

Listen and practise contrasting the syllable lengths in these words.

Longer vowel		*Shorter vowel*
her	heard	hurt
lay	laid	late
pea	peas	peace
rye	rise	rice
fee	feed	feet
sir	surge	search

Check your progress

First, listen and repeat:

excuse me
excuse me, please
eyes
with my eyes
lens
is it a lens?
use
it's no use
eyes
close your eyes
safe
is that safe?
fizz
Bucks fizz

Listen to the dialogue.

A: Will you excuse me, please. There's something wrong with my eyes.
B: Is it a lens?
A: No, I think it's dust ... It's no use!
B: Close your eyes and put some ice over them.
A: Is that safe?
B: Of course. Here, use the ice from my Bucks fizz.

Now practise the dialogue with a partner. Practise until you can say it without reading.

20 Stops and continuants

Besides voicing, another basic distinction between consonants is whether they are stop sounds or continuant sounds. Practise feeling the difference.

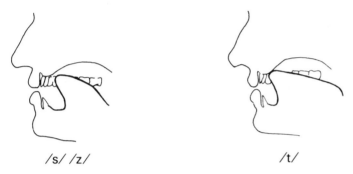

/s/ /z/   /t/

Say 'is' and hold the 's' sound as long as you can. That is a continuant sound. Now say 'it'. Can you hold the 't'? You can't hold it because 't' is a stop sound.

Is the sound 'th' a stop or a continuant?

The sounds of English

	Stops		Continuants
Voiced	<u>b</u>ay, <u>d</u>ip game		<u>v</u>ine, <u>z</u>ip, <u>th</u>is, mea<u>s</u>ure, <u>l</u>ow, <u>r</u>ow, <u>m</u>ow, <u>n</u>o
		<u>j</u>eep*	
Unvoiced	<u>p</u>ay, <u>t</u>ip, <u>c</u>ame	<u>ch</u>eap*	<u>f</u>ine, <u>s</u>ip, <u>th</u>in, me<u>sh</u>

* The 'j' and 'ch' sounds at the beginning of these words have an initial stop ('d' and 't' respectively) and then a continuant sound.

Part 1: Pronunciation

A 🔲

1 Listen and underline the word you hear in the recorded sentences.

    1 a) soup b) Sue
    2 a) watching b) washing
    3 a) fine b) pine
    4 a) taught b) thought
    5 a) dam b) ram

2 Now listen to the recorded sentences and choose the appropriate reply. Put a cross by it.

    1 Reply: a) It's too hot! ....
               b) It's too heavy! ....
    2 Reply: a) Me too. Especially with steak. ....
               b) I don't, I get seasick. ....
    3 Reply: a) The fifth of November. ....
               b) It's Friday. ....
    4 Reply: a) Well, you shouldn't gamble. ....
               b) Mm, it's expensive keeping pets. ....
    5 Reply: a) No, it's orange. ....
               b) No, it's alive. ....

B 🔲

1 Listen to these words. Which of the columns of words ends in continuant sounds? Practise saying both groups.

1	*2*
have	cab
teethe	made
eyes	bag
half	cap
teeth	mate
ice	back

2 Now listen and practise contrasting stop and continuant endings.

wife	wipe
both	boat
bath	bat
loathe	load
rove	robe

82

C 🔲

We have already seen how sounds change and words link together in natural speech (Units 7 and 8). When a word ends in a consonant, the final sounds often changes in order to link that word more easily to the next one. When the final consonant of a word is the same as the initial consonant of the next word, the two consonants 'merge'.

Listen to these groups of linked words and practise saying them. Don't sound the first consonant, sound the second. This consonant takes more time.

Continuant–to–continuant:
Richard, give Vera a drink.
Tim, don't push Sheila.
And don't pull Linda's hair!
Vera, give Thomas some too!

Stop–to–stop:
Diane, please stop pushing!
Now you've hurt Thomas!
Did Richard do that?
Quick, bring Greg a cloth!

D 🔲

We saw in Unit 7 how consonants can reduce or weaken in rapid speech to avoid a difficult group of sounds. This is particularly common with stop sounds at the end of a word or before a stressed syllable, when they are hardly pronounced.

Listen to this sentence and underline the 't' and 'k' sounds that are not actually pronounced.

'I like those black boots but I think that white jacket looks ghastly!'

Now listen and repeat.

ghastly
looks ghastly
jacket
white jacket
that white jacket
that white jacket looks ghastly
I think
I think that white jacket looks ghastly

boots
black boots
I like
I like those black boots

I like those black boots but I think that white jacket looks ghastly!

21 Puff of air (aspiration)

The sounds 'p', 't' and 'k' (unvoiced stops) have an extra signal to distinguish them clearly from 'b', 'd' and 'g' (voiced stops). This signal is an extra puff of air.

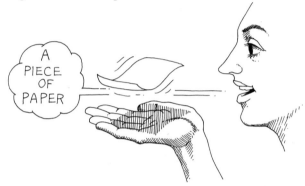

If you hold a piece of paper in front of your mouth you can test yourself. The paper should move when you say a voiceless stop with a puff of air. The paper will not move without the puff of air. You can also test yourself by holding your hand in front of your mouth. You should feel the difference between the presence and absence of the puff of air.

A

Practise adding the puff of air.

oo ... too   ee ... tea
eye ... pie   ay ... pay
old ... cold   ow ... cow

Rule: the unvoiced stops ('p', 't' and 'k') have an extra puff of air:
a) at the beginning of a word;
b) before a clear vowel;
(except when preceded by an 's').

Note: Remember that stops are not pronounced clearly at the end of words or unstressed syllables in rapid, natural speech.

B 〔⋯〕

Listen and then practise making the difference between these words:

buy   pie
bet   pet
down   town
done   ton
game   came
good   could

C 〔⋯〕

1 Listen and underline the word you hear in the recorded sentences:
   1 a) try   b) dry
   2 a) Poppy   b) Bobby
   3 a) curls   b) girls
   4 a) goat   b) coat
   5 a) drunk   b) trunk

2 Now listen to the recorded sentences and choose the appropriate
   reply. Put a cross by it.

   1 Reply: a) No, it's silver.   ....
            b) No, it's hot.   ....
   2 Reply: a) Let's go to another.   ....
            b) Maybe it's hungry.   ....
   3 Reply: a) Mm, it's ripe and juicy.   ....
            b) Yes, just look at the sand.   ....
   4 Reply: a) In the bathroom.   ....
            b) At the end of the village.   ....
   5 Reply: a) Yes, I never take them unless I'm really ill.   ....
            b) Yes, I never pay them unless I really have to.   ....

D 〔⋯〕

Listen and repeat.

please
passports please
pocket
in my pocket
put it in my pocket
perhaps
perhaps I put it in my pocket

》》→

typical
it's typical
to tell you
I tried to tell you
It's typical! I tried to tell you.

car
in the car
Gatwick Airport
coming
coming to Gatwick Airport
coming to Gatwick Airport in the car
out
got it out
I got it out when we were coming to Gatwick Airport in the car.

plane
on the plane
put
I put that on the plane ...

Listen to the dialogue.

A: Passports please.
B: I can't quite remember where ...
C: What did you do with it?
B: Perhaps I put it in my pocket.
C: It's typical! I tried to tell you.
B: Goodness! I remember. I got it out when we were coming to
   Gatwick Airport in the car and ... gave it to you!
C: To me!
B: Perhaps you put it in your big black bag.
C: But I put that on the plane when we checked in!
B: Oh.

Check your progress

Practise the dialogue with a partner and then record it.

22 Review

In the previous units you have practised making some essential sound contrasts in English:
1 Voiced/unvoiced sounds, e.g. 's', 'z' and 'p', 'b', and length of syllables, e.g. 'cap', 'cab'.
2 Stops and continuants, e.g. 't', 'th'.
3 Puff of air, e.g. 'p', 't', 'k'.

Now try these exercises.

A Voicing and length of syllables 📼

Listen and then practise the following words. Lengthen the vowel before the final voiced sound.

Long	Short	Long	Short
save	safe	use (verb)	use (noun)
service	surface	prove (verb)	proof (noun)
rode	wrote	close (verb)	close (adj.)
bed	bet	lose (verb)	loose (adj.)
heard	hurt		

B Contrast between stops and continuants 📼

Listen to these sentences and then practise saying them.

1 Dan ran out of the dentist's and rushed directly to the doctor's.
2 Tania thinks they teach that theory too much.

C Puff of air 📼

Listen to these word pairs and then practise saying them.

pan ... ban	tie ... die	came ... game
pole ... bowl	toe ... dough	could ... good
pace ... base	tense ... dense	cash ... gash

23 Sound contrasts – Consonants

Diagnostic test

See if you can recognise some of these sound contrasts.

🔲 Listen to the recorded dialogue. Two people are trying to read a list of people's names, but the writing is not very clear. What do they decide? Put a cross by the appropriate name.

Example:
A: I think his name is Vane, John Vane.
B: No, it's not, it's Wane.

1 John Vane   ....
  John Wane   ....×.......

2 Alan Riddle   ....
  Alan Liddle   ....
3 June Varley   ....
  June Barley   ....
4 Anna Poulton   ....
  Anna Foulton   ....
5 Eric Litham   ....
  Eric Littam   ....
6 Erika Siegler ....
  Erika Ziegler ....
7 Jonathan Shepstow   ....
  Jonathan Chepstow   ....
8 Sue Arlington   ....
  Sue Harlington ....

If you had problems recognising some of these sounds, turn to the appropriate section in this unit for further practice.

1 'th' / 't'

It is important to distinguish between the pronunciation of the letters 'th' and 't'. Also the letters 'th' can be produced as two different sounds: voiced and unvoiced.

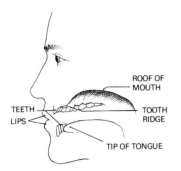 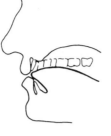 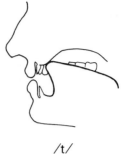

ROOF OF
MOUTH

TEETH
LIPS

TOOTH
RIDGE

TIP OF TONGUE

/th/   /t/

A

Listen and practise the difference in these words.

	Continuants	*Stops*
Voiced	they	day
	than	Dan
	those	doze
	loathe	load
Unvoiced	thought	taught
	thank	tank
	thin	tin
	theme	team
	bath	bat
	both	boat

B

Say the words below and ask a partner to put them in the correct group above.

dare	bad	clothes	breath
there	din	that	month
toes	these	teeth	breathe

C

Practise saying these phrases, concentrating on the clarity of the 'th' and 't' sounds.

What's the time?   On both sides.
Who's that?   In three months' time.
Those three.

2 'th' / 's' / 'z'

We have seen that the letters 'th' can be pronounced in two different ways: voiced and unvoiced. The letter 's', similarly, can be produced as two different sounds: voiced and unvoiced. A voiced 's' is the same sound as a 'z'.

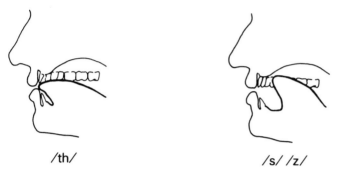

/th/   /s/ /z/

A

Listen and then practise the difference in saying these words. With a partner, take turns testing each other.

	1	*2*
Voiced	then	Zen
	clothe	close
	clothing	closing
Unvoiced	thin	sin
	thought	sought
	thank	sank

B

Practise asking the questions and choosing the correct answers.

Questions	*Answers*
What's this?	These are zips.
Who's that?	Those are zebra.
What are these?	That's Zoë.
What are those?	This is a zoo.

3 'sh' / 'ch' / 'j'

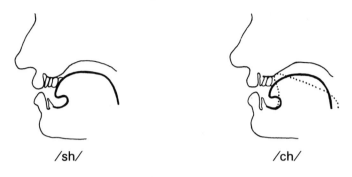

/sh/   /ch/

The 'ch' sound is a combination of 't' (a stop) and then 'sh' (a continuant). The contrast between 'ch' and 'sh' is a contrast between a combined stop-continuant and a simple continuant.

To make a 'j' sound, say 'ch' but change the initial 't' to 'd'.

A

Listen and then practise the difference in these words.

1	2	3
share	chair	jaw
shoe	chew	Jew
sheep	cheap	jeep
dish	ditch	ridge
cash	catch	cadge

B

Say these words quickly and ask a partner to put them in the correct column above.

cheque	shells	jam
cheese	chance	chin
shoes	sugar	station
choose	China	major
ginger	rich	

4 'v' / 'b'

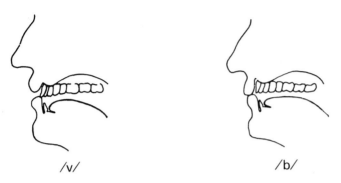

/v/   /b/

A

Listen and then practise saying these contrasts. Make sure you close your lips for 'b'.

vet	bet
van	ban
very	berry
vote	boat

B

Practise reading this dialogue with a partner, making a clear contrast between 'v' and 'b'.

A: This van is going very fast.
B: Yes, I bet he's over the speed limit.
A: The police can ban you from driving for a year.
B: That would be very unfortunate.
A: Yes. I vote we tell him to stop.

5 'v' / 'w'

Make a 'v' sound (see the illustration opposite), making sure your top teeth touch your bottom lip. Now make a 'w', making sure your lips do not touch your teeth. (Try making a 'u' and then changing to a 'i', and gradually speed up.)

A

Listen and practise these contrasts.

1	2
vet	wet
veal	wheel
vine	wine
veil	whale
vest	west

Now say the words above in any order. Get your partner or teacher to tell you which column they are in.

B

Practise saying the following sentences with a partner, and giving the correct responses.

1 A: There's something wrong with this a) veal.
        b) wheel.
    B: c) It should be fresh.
         d) Ask the garage to check it.

2 A: This is a very old a) vine.
        b) wine.
    B: c) When was it planted?
         d) It's delicious.

C

Listen and practise saying this sentence.

'There were many Viking villages in various parts of north-east and west England, and there are still words in our language with Scandinavian origins.'

6 'h'

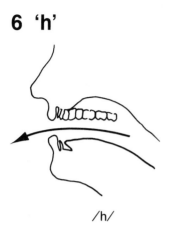

/h/

It is important to pronounce the 'h' sound clearly at the beginning of stressed syllables (although it is commonly reduced in unstressed syllables and words).

A 🔲

Listen and practise making the difference between these pairs of words.

1	*2*
eye	high
art	heart
air	hair
and	hand
arm	harm
eight	hate

Say the words above in any order. Get your partner or teacher to tell you which column they are in.

B 🔲

There are some words where 'h' is not pronounced. Listen and practise saying them.

(h)our	(h)onest
(h)eir	g(h)ost
g(h)astly	ex(h)aust
ve(h)icle	ex(h)ibition

C

Listen to the dialogue and put a line through the silent/reduced 'h's in it.

Example: Is ~~h~~e hurt?

A: Hello, Helen.
B: Hello, Alan. How's Harry?
A: Haven't you heard? He's had an accident in the house.
B: Has he? Is he hurt?
A: Well, he's gone to hospital in an ambulance. Apparently, he's having an operation on his hip.
B: How awful. I hope he's all right.
A: I hope so too.

Now practise reading the dialogue with a partner. Make sure you say the 'h' clearly in stressed syllables, but not when they are reduced or silent.

Note: Make sure you make the necessary links between words, e.g. 'He's had an accident.' This will help you NOT to put in an 'h' sound where there isn't one!

7 'p' / 'b'

The 'b' sound is made like 'p', but is voiced.

A

Listen and practise saying these contrasts.

1	*2*
bat	pat
bowl	pole
boot	put
beach	peach
bin	pin
beat	Pete
cub	cup

B

Ask another student to tell you whether you said (a) or (b).

1 a) Can you bring me that large pole?
   b) Can you bring me that large bowl?
2 a) It's a fine beach.
   b) It's a fine peach.
3 a) I need a pin.
   b) I need a bin.

8 'r' / 'l'

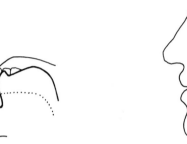
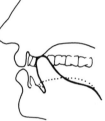

Two steps to 'r'
1 Say 'ahhh' … (dotted line in illustration).
2 Continue saying 'ah', and curl tongue tip back (solid line).

Two steps to 'l'
1 Say 'ahhh' … (dotted line in illustration).
2 Continue saying 'ah', and reach tongue tip forward (solid line).

Notice the difference in the position of the lips.

A ⌣

Listen and then practise these sounds slowly until you can say them with a clear contrast.

1 a ram, a lamb, a ram, a lamb
2 a reef, a leaf, a reef, a leaf
3 a road, a load, a road, a load
4 arrive, alive, arrive, alive
5 pirate, pilot, pirate, pilot
6 clash, crash, clash, crash
7 pray, play, pray, play
8 right, light, right, light

B

Put the words below into rows with the same sound. Then practise saying them.
Example:

1	2	3
red	led	dead

ray, lie, lay, low, die, row, room, rye, doom, dead, deep, loom, dough, day, reap, led, red, leap

C

Listen to the recorded sentences and choose the correct reply. Put a cross by it.

1 Reply: a) No, it's wrong. ....
        b) No, it's dark. ....
2 Reply: a) Yes, I've been gardening. ....
        b) Mind you don't cut yourself. ....
3 Reply: a) Yes, look at its horns! ....
        b) Ah. It looks very young. ....

D

Listen and then repeat.

Roger
Hello, Roger
How's life?
Hello, Roger. How's life?

really
Oh, really!
Florence
in Florence
last year
last year in Florence
married
got married
We got married last year in Florence.

librarian
still a librarian
Are you still a librarian?

97

a drink
for a drink
round
come round
Come round for a drink sometime.

Now listen to the dialogue.

A: Hello, Roger. How's life?
B: Oh, all right. How's Laura?
A: Fine, fine. She's a lawyer now, you know.
B: Oh, really! Are you two married then?
A: Yes. We got married last year in Florence.
B: Oh, lovely!
A: What about you, Roger? Are you still a librarian?
B: Yeah. Still the same old job. It's pretty boring actually.
A: Well, come round for a drink sometime. Laura still talks about you.
B: Really! Well ...

Now practise the dialogue with a partner.

Check your progress ☺

Listen to the conversation and complete the diary with one of the names from each of the pairs below.

1 a) Mr Arkwright
  b) Mr Harkwright
2 a) Miss Fane
  b) Miss Vane
3 a) Mr Booze
  b) Mr Booth
4 a) Mrs Witherson
  b) Mrs Widderson
5 a) Miss Rishley
  b) Miss Ritchley

Wednesday	**14 July**
9.15	
10.00	
10.30	
11.15	
11.45	

24 Sound contrasts – Vowels

Diagnostic test 📼

Try this test to see if you have any difficulties with the basic English vowel contrasts.

1 Listen to the recorded groups of words (there are sixteen). Pick out the word which sounds different in each group of four. Write down whether it is A, B, C or D.

	A	B	C	D
Example:	bean	bean	bean	<u>bun</u>

2 Now listen to the recorded sentences and choose the appropriate response. Put a cross by it.

1 a) Oh, don't worry, it's nothing serious. ....
  b) Of course, it's only a kitten really. ....

2 a) No, just a few. ....
  b) Well ... yes, £10. ....

3 a) No, it's still free. ....
  b) No, it was broken. ....

4 a) No, it's a boy. ....
  b) No, it's a pigeon. ....

5 a) Certainly sir, how many nights? ....
  b) Certainly sir, straight or with coke? ....

6 a) Well, there was a no-parking sign! ....
  b) Mm, it's a dangerous horse. ....

⟫→

Part 1

The diagrams below show the position of the tongue for three contrasting vowels.

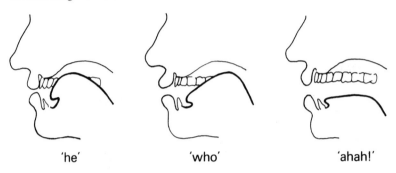

'he'   'who'   'ahah!'

A 😐

Now listen and then practise saying the following words and notice how the lips and tongue move.

tea ... two (tongue moves backwards)
tea ... tar (tongue moves down)
tar ... two (tongue moves up)
two ... tea (tongue moves forwards)

B 😐

The diagram below shows the relationship between English vowels, according to the position of the highest point of the tongue.

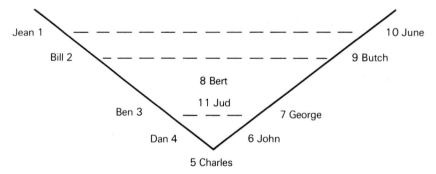

Listen to the eleven different vowel sounds.
   Now practise saying them as you listen. What happens to your jaw between sound 1 and sound 6?

C

Listen to the contrast of vowel 11 and all the other vowels.

1	beat	11	but
2	bit		but
3	bet		but
4	bat		but
5	bart		but
6	bot		but
7	bought		but
8	bert		but
9	book		but
10	boot		but

D

Practice the vowel sounds in 'Jean' and 'Bill'. Listen to the recorded groups of words (there are seven). Pick out the word which sounds different in each group of four. Write down whether it is A, B, C or D.

	A	B	C	D
Example:	seek	seek	seek	<u>sick</u>

E

Listen and then practise saying these sounds. Notice some of their possible spellings.

'Jean'	*'Bill'*
feet	sip
sleep	kit
seem	little
steal	pill
teach	picnic
speak	syllable
theme	symbol
Pete	myth
thief	busy
belief	pretty

F ⌷

Listen to the recorded questions and choose the appropriate response. Put a cross by it.

1 a) In a hotel. ....
  b) On the ice. ....
2 a) At two o'clock. ....
  b) In the 19th century. ....
3 a) Yes, I'm coming. ....
  b) Yes, we're all here. ....

Part 2

Sometimes vowel sounds are put together to form 'diphthongs'. These sounds are usually longer than simple vowel sounds.

G ⌷

1 Listen to these vowels.

bay   Tay
buy   tie
boy   toy

Now practise saying them as you listen. Your tongue should finish in the same position for each vowel.

2 Now practise contrasting the sounds in column 1 and column 2. The sounds in column 1 are longer than the sounds in column 2.

1	*2*
fail	fell
fight	fat
join	John

H ⌷

1 Listen to these vowels.

tier   pier
tear   pear
tour   poor

Now practise saying them as you listen. Your tongue should finish in the same position for each vowel.

2 Now practise contrasting the sounds in column 1 and column 2.

1	2
pier	pea
fairy	ferry
sure	shoe

I ☺

1 Listen to these vowels.

no	sew
now	sow

Now practise saying them as you listen. Your tongue should finish in the same position for each vowel.

2 Now practise contrasting the sounds in column 1 and column 2.

1	2
phone	fun
town	tan

J ☺

Now practise some vowel contrasts in context. First, listen and repeat.

morning
good morning
Fairless
Boyd
Boyd and Fairless
Boyd and Fairless, good morning

Service
After Sales
After Sales Service

through
put me through
could you put me through

Carstairs
my name's Carstairs

moment
at the moment

busy
busy at the moment
Mr Fewster
Mr Fewster is busy at the moment

help me
who could help me
someone else
is there
is there someone else
Well, is there someone else who could help me?

important
quite important
this is quite important
look
Look, this is quite important.

Listen to the dialogue.

A: Boyd and Fairless, good morning.
B: Good morning. I'd like to speak to the person in charge of your After Sales Service, please.
A: That's Mr Fewster.
B: Could you put me through to him, please?
A: Who's speaking, please?
B: My name's Carstairs.
A: Just a moment, Mr Carstairs ... I'm sorry Mr Carstairs, Mr Fewster is busy at the moment.
B: Well, is there someone else who could help me?
A: There's Mrs Parsons. She's the assistant manager ...
B: Fine.
A: But she's out at the moment.

B: Look, this is quite important!
A: I'll try Mr Fewster's line again for you.
B: Thank you.
A: Trying to connect you.
B: Ah! Is that Mr Fewster? Good morning, this is ... Hello? ...
   Hello? ... Oh no!

Now practise the dialogue with a partner.

Check your progress

Now see if you can distinguish between vowel sounds in context.
Look at the map and then listen to the woman in the tourist
information office telling a tourist where places are. Listen and write
the correct number by the buildings on the map.
Example:
Tourist officer: Here you are, sir, the bank is in Fane Street.   (1a)

These are the buildings:

1 the bank   5 the museum
2 the post office   6 the Red Line (pub)
3 the chemist   7 the Red Lion (pub)
4 the library

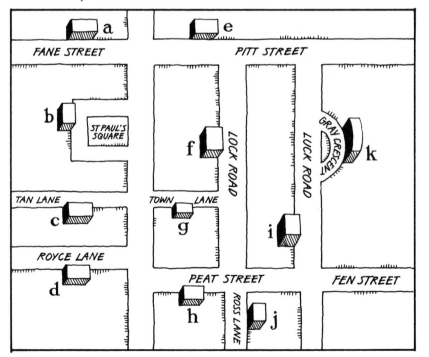

PART 2: LISTENING

Introduction

This part of the book concentrates on listening skills. You will use some of the information you have already studied in the first part to help you listen more *accurately* and *efficiently* to a variety of authentic and semi-authentic recordings.

Listening *accurately* means:
– knowing what to expect to hear;
– recognising elements of natural, connected speech;
– being able to hear different sounds;
– being able to segment the sounds into words.

Listening *efficiently* means:
– being able to distinguish between important and unimportant information (i.e. 'get the gist');
– making use of context to guess, predict and interpret meaning;
– being able to follow the structure of talk (i.e. 'keep track').

Listening difficulties

A

Do you think any of the following elements cause you difficulties when listening to English speakers? If so, which ones?

unfamiliar subject
unfamiliar accent
unfamiliar vocabulary
number of speakers (interruptions, speaking together)
concentration over long periods (get words but lose ideas)
elements of connected speech:
- too fast (few pauses, unfamiliar rhythm, etc.)
- don't recognise familiar words/phrases (reductions, contractions, linking, etc.)

B

Now listen to the three recorded extracts of natural speech and decide which is the easiest to understand.
1 'Students in Nice'
2 'Marriage'
3 'Boxing'

C 📟

Listen again to each extract and complete the table below:

Extracts:	1	2	3
Type of speech: a) dialogue b) group discussion c) unfamiliar subject d) unfamiliar accent e) unfamiliar vocabulary f) fast	✓	✓	✓
Clarity of speech: g) clear pauses h) clear stress i) clear focus j) hesitations k) unfinished sentences			

Name: .... Date: ....
Nationality: ....

Listening test 😐

Part 1: Listening accuracy

This section tests your ability to:
a) discriminate sounds;
b) discriminate words in speech.

A

This is an extract from an interview about boxing and snooker.

1 Listen to the complete extract once.

2 Listen to the extract again, short sections at a time, and decide
which words, (a) or (b), are actually said.

'There must be, for both of you, | a) a feeling, | I mean | a) do you
| b) a kind of feeling, | | b) don't you

| get a lot of people | a) saying, | "Well, boxing and snooker | a) wasn't
| b) say, | | b) isn't

| what it used to be when it | a) wasn't quite so glamorous." |
| b) was quite glamorous." |

Do you get | a) that | kind of | a) comments | a lot?'
| b) those | | b) comment |

B

1 Listen to the complete extract once.
2 Listen again, to short sections at a time, and write down exactly
what you hear.

....

....

....

....

© Cambridge University Press 1990   109

Part 2: Listening comprehension 1

This section tests your ability to:
a) 'get the message', i.e. get key information;
b) ignore unimportant information.

C

1 Listen to the complete recording once only.
2 Write down the message in the minimum number of words necessary.

Messages

To: ....

From: ....

Message: ....

....

....

....

....

Tel No: ....

Part 3: Listening comprehension 2

This section tests your ability to:
a) understand main ideas;
b) follow the 'thread' or structure;
c) recognise pronunciation 'signals' in context.

D

Understanding main ideas. You are going to hear part of a discussion about how foreigners living in France can choose to educate their children.
1 Listen to the complete recording once.

                                    © Cambridge University Press 1990

2 Choose the best response to each of the following:
  1 The speaker's main idea is:
    a) It is easier for younger children to become bilingual. ☐
    b) There are two main factors to consider in deciding on the type of school. ☐
    c) France has got the best system of nursery schools in Europe. ☐

  2 When talking about the 'younger child' the speaker doesn't mention one of the following factors:
    a) Children can start nursery school at the age of two in France. ☐
    b) It is easier for young children to become bilingual. ☐
    c) Younger children don't notice cultural differences. ☐

  3 When talking about the 'older child' the speaker mentions which of the following factors first?
    a) The problem of qualifications. ☐
    b) The problem of adjusting to the system. ☐
    c) The length of time spent in the foreign country. ☐

E

Following the 'thread'. Listen to the recording from Exercise D again without stopping the tape. Write notes to record the important information. Use the chart below as a guide.

Educating foreign children in France

Choice of .... – main factors:

1 ....

2 ....

Recommendations for 'younger child':

....

because:

....

Recommendations for '............................... child':

....

because:

1 ....

2 ....

© Cambridge University Press 1990

F

Recognising pronunciation 'signals'. Listen to this extract again:

'The first is the age of the child and the second is the way the parents perceive what are two very different educational traditions.'

Now answer these questions:
1 The speaker divides the sentence into two parts. Where?
2 What is the 'focus' (i.e. the most important) word in the first part?
3 In the second part the word 'perceive' is given extra stress. Why?
4 Does the speaker's voice finish high or low on 'traditions'? Why?

© Cambridge University Press 1990

25 Listening accuracy 1

A

Listen to the telephone message that has been recorded on an answering machine.

Listen to the message again and make notes. You only want the most important information so write content words only.
Example:

> ## Message
>
> From: .....*Jan*...
>
> ....*Can't meet lunch* . . . .
>
> ....
>
> ....

B

Now listen to the message again. This time it is read as a dictation.
After each bleep, pause the tape and write the message.

C 📼

Check the accuracy of what you have written.

1 Did you get all the content words right?
2 Did you miss some reduced words, e.g. articles (the), prepositions (on, to, at)? If they are missing here, they will probably be missing from your English, spoken and written. This will affect the rhythm of your spoken English and will make your writing less effective.
3 Can you make the necessary connections between pronunciation and spelling? If you have trouble with this you should practise listening while you read.

26 Listening accuracy 2

A woman is discussing her holiday plans with a travel agent.

A

Look carefully at the booking form. Are you familiar with all the vocabulary? If not, check in a dictionary.

FREETIME HOLIDAYS	BOOKING FORM				
HOLIDAY REF:	DEPARTURE DATE		NO. OF NIGHTS		
PASSENGER'S NAME					
Mr/Mrs Ms/Miss	Initials	Surname	Address		
			Phone (home)		
			(work)		
DESTINATION/TOUR					
HOTEL/APARTMENT/VILLA					
ACCOMMODATION	Standard room	Superior room	Deluxe room	Studio apartment	Other
Single					
Twin					
Triple					
MEAL PLAN	Room only	Room/breakfast		Half Board	Full Board
COST					
Per person					
SUPPLEMENTS	Accommodation		Meals	Departure date	Other
Total price					
DEPOSIT Enclosed please find deposit of		CREDIT CARDS Card No. .... I wish to pay by credit card. Signature			

B 🔲

Listen to the conversation between the woman and the travel agent. Listen especially for the items on the booking form.

C 🔲

Listen to the conversation again. This time, try to complete the booking form yourself. Listen to the conversation as many times as you want.

27 Getting key information 1

Listen to the recorded travel announcements and complete the charts below.

A

At the airport

```
┌─────────────────────────────────────┐
│ BRITISH                             │
│ AIRWAYS    Departures               │
│ Flight No: ........................ │
│ Destination: ...................... │
│ Departure time: ................... │
│ Delay: ............................ │
│                                     │
│ Passenger instructions:            │
│ 1 ................................. │
│ 2 ................................. │
└─────────────────────────────────────┘
```

B

At the railway station

ARRIVALS	DEPARTURES
Time:	Time: ....
To:	To: ....
Platform:	Platform: ....

C

Listen to this announcement on a train and decide if these statements are true or false.

1 There is a buffet car on the train.
2 It is situated at the rear of second class.
3 It sells soft drinks.
4 It will close in 25 minutes.

TRUE	FALSE

28   Getting key information 2

Several people were asked where places were in, or near, York Railway Station, in England.

A

You will hear these words in the recording. Check any new words in a dictionary.

ticket barrier
left luggage office
facing
next door

B   ⌷⌷

Look at the plan of York Railway Station opposite. Listen to the recording once through, without stopping the tape.

Listen again, and write the correct number by the places on the plan. Listen to the tape as often as you need to.

These are the places:
1 ladies' toilet
2 left luggage office
3 car park
4 bus station

C   ⌷⌷

Listen again. This time listen particularly to the questions. What are the two main question patterns that you hear?

1 Excuse me. .... ?
2 Excuse me. .... ?

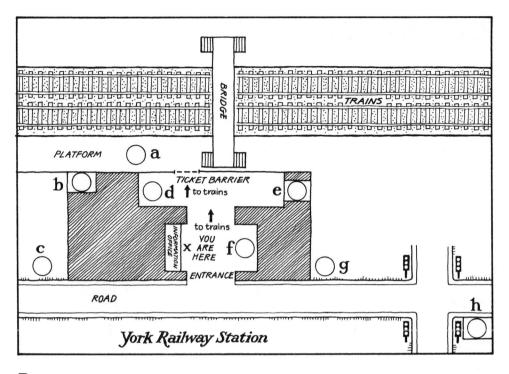

D 😐

1 Listen to the dialogue about the car park again. Complete the second speaker's sentence:

- Excuse me. Is there a car park near the station?
- Yes, as you're .... the station, it's
  ....

2 Listen to the dialogue about the bus station again. Complete the second speaker's instructions:

- Excuse me. Could you tell me where the bus station is?
- Yes, certainly. If you go out of the station, ... to your left. .... the road down to .... You'll see it ....

29 Review

Three people were asked about their work.

A

You will hear these words in the recording. Check any new words in a dictionary.

to print
a post-graduate student
a soap opera
to hang around
live performance
audience feedback
to record
bands
sound effects
to end up with
on the audio side

B

Listen once to the three speakers and decide which of the photographs represent their present jobs.

1   2

3 4

5 6

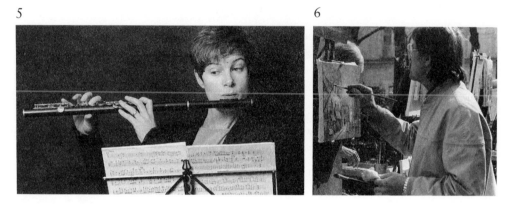

Ann-Marie's present job: ....

John's present job: ....

Dave's present job: ....

C ⌣

Now listen to the first interview again, with Ann-Marie. Fill in the information:

1 She works in a .... in the ....
She has done this job in York for .... years.
She was a(n) .... in .... for a year.

2 Listen to the last part of the interview again. Ann-Marie said:

'I taught English in Sweden for a year.'

She divided this sentence into three thought groups. Decide where the end of the thought groups could be and put a pause mark (/) between the words. Can you hear the pauses?

D ☐

Now listen to the second interview again, with John. Fill in the information:

1 John said: 'I work on a .... basis.'
   Which of these does this mean?
   a) He works voluntarily (i.e. without pay).
   b) He is not qualified.
   c) He is self-employed, i.e. he has no employer.

2 He acts mostly:
   a) on the stage
   b) in films
   c) on TV

3 He prefers acting .... because he gets .... from he audience.

E ☐

Now listen to the third interview again, with Dave. Fill in the information:

1 He has been in his present job for .... years.
   Before that he was ...., and played the .... and
   ....
   He has made a few ...., and been .... a lot.

2 Listen to the beginning of the interview again. Dave said:

   'I'm a recording engineer.'

   a) Which is the first stressed word in that sentence?
   b) There are two syllables which have the most emphasis, which ones are they?

3 Listen to the end of the interview again. Dave said:

   'I also worked in electronics, and I worked on the audio side.'

   Find two other examples of this pattern: 'the .... side'.

30   Taking notes 1

This is the first of two units on note-taking techniques. You will hear a short lecture about note-taking skills.

A ⌸

Listen to the whole talk once through for general comprehension, and answer these questions.

1 How many reasons were there to explain that taking notes in a foreign language is difficult?
2 How many skills were mentioned to help you take better notes?

B ⌸

Now listen again and make notes using this chart as a guide.

Reason for taking notes: ....

Difficulties in taking notes:
1 ....
2 ....
3 ....

Important skills to help take better notes:
1 ....
2 .... (e.g. ....) and
   .... (e.g. ....)
3 .... (e.g. ....)

C

When you have finished, check what you have written. Did you get all the main ideas? Did you hear the content and focus words? Did you hear the low pitch to mark the end of an idea and high pitch to mark a new idea?

31 Taking notes 2

You will hear a short lecture describing some recent research about learning the pronunciation of a foreign language.

A

Can you think of any reasons why some students seem to have better pronunciation in a foreign language than others?

B ☺

Listen to the talk and choose one answer to each of the following questions.

1 The main idea of the talk is:
   a) Attitudes to pronunciation make a difference to pronunciation learning.
   b) Outgoing people are not better at pronunciation than shy people.
   c) Several factors influence students' pronunciation achievement.

2 The talk claimed that:
   a) The student's mother tongue is the most significant factor in pronunciation learning.
   b) Natural ability is not a significant factor in pronunciation learning.
   c) Women learn pronunciation better than men.

3 Which of the following possible explanations was not mentioned?
   a) It is easier to learn a language closer to one's own.
   b) A positive attitude towards pronunciation improves learning.
   c) Children learn pronunciation better than adults.

C ☺

Now listen to the talk again and take notes. When you have finished, check what you have written. Did you get all the important ideas? Are your notes easy to read? Do they consist mainly of content words?

32 Following structure

In this unit you will hear two versions of a presentation about a private language school – Clifton Language Training.

A

You will hear these words in the recordings. Check any new vocabulary in a dictionary.

an analysis of needs   a consultancy   thorough
to run a course   on-site   follow-up
to commission   freelance   evaluation

B

Before you listen to the recordings, try to decide what you think makes a good oral presentation.

C ☐

Listen to both presentations. Try to answer these questions.

1 What is Clifton Language Training?
2 Where is Clifton?
3 How many partners are there?
4 What is ESP?
5 What sorts of courses are run?
6 What else does Clifton Language Training do, apart from run courses for students?
7 What is the general sequence of events in running a specific English language course?

How many questions were you able to answer by the end of the first presentation?
What did you think were the main differences between the two presentations?

D ☒

Look at the listener's checklist. Now listen to both presentations again but, this time, note down your reaction to the different aspects of the talks. Note examples of good points or weak points.

Listener's checklist

Write '1' (for Presentation 1) and '2' (for Presentation 2) in the appropriate column.

	Yes	OK	No
1 Did the speaker make it easy for the listener to understand?			
2 Was the amount of information correct?			

3 *Structure*
  a) Was there an 'introduction', 'middle' and 'conclusion'?
  b) Was there a clear sequence to help predict what would come next?			

4 *Speech*
  a) Were there clear:
   – focus words / stress?
   – thought groups / pauses?
   – pitch changes?
  b) Were there many hesitations and 'fillers'?
  c) Was there correct:
   – volume?
   – speed?			

E ☒

The use of *pauses* and *stress* is very important for a good presentation.

Listen to this extract from Presentation 2:

'There are FIVE PARtners / FOUR TEAching partners / and ONE adMINistrative partner / and / in adDItion / there are several experienced FREElance teachers.'

(/ = pause; capitals, e.g. FIVE = stress)

Pauses give the audience time to:
a) digest what has just been said;
b) anticipate what will be said next;
c) see which words go together to form thought groups.

Stress helps the audience focus on the most important information in a sentence.

The extract below has no punctuation. Punctuation, in written language, does what pauses and stress do in spoken language. Read the extract and mark where you think the main pauses and stress come (as in the extract above).

'so firstly what is Clifton Language Training well it's an English language training consultancy based in Clifton in the north of England it was established in 1980 with the objective of specialising in industry-specific language training there are principally two main activities'

Now listen to the extract and check whether you were right.

33   Keeping track

You are going to hear part of an interview with some British and American students who are currently studying at the University of Nice in the south of France. They are giving their opinions about living and studying in France.

A

You will hear these words in the recording. Check any new vocabulary in a dictionary.

fluent
abroad
prior

B

What do you think are some of the advantages and disadvantages of studying and living in a foreign country?

C

Listen to the complete recording once. Do the students reply positively or negatively to the following questions?

	Yes	No
1 Will any of the students return to France later?		
2 Has their French improved?		
3 Is France an easier place to live than the UK?		

D ⌣

There are several times when people speak at the same time or interrupt each other, so consequently there are unfinished sentences.

Listen again for the sentences below and try to predict how the speaker intended to finish them:

1 'Compared to the length of time we studied in England and how much we improved there, it's amazing ....,'
2 'It's the only way to do it really, to become really fluent in a language ....,'
3 'Do you think France is an easier place to live than Britain (I'll ask the Brits first and then the Americans) at the moment? I mean, do you think it's ....,'

E ⌣

Listen to the recording again and write down the exact questions the interviewer asks. There are five questions.

Then decide if he is 'checking' or 'getting' information each time.

34 Review

The recording is part of a radio interview with Patrick Middleton, a lecturer in sociology. He is giving his views about marriage.

A

You will hear these words in the recording. Check any new vocabulary in a dictionary.

average
a stretch
divorce rate
life span

B

Do you think people's idea of marriage is changing? Are the marriage and divorce rates stable in your country?

C ⌷

Listen to the complete recording once through to try and get a general understanding of Patrick's explanations.

The main points he is making are that:
a) Marriage is longer than it was 100 years ago.
b) Marriage is changing.
c) People have fewer children than they used to.

D ⌷

Listen again, to short sections at a time, and take notes of the main and supporting ideas Patrick gives. Use the chart to help you.

Main idea:	Marriage ....
	especially in terms of ....
Supporting ideas:	e.g. 100 years ago ....
	because: a) .... later
	b) .... earlier
	Marriage was ....
	i.e. shorter with ....
	therefore, ...
Main idea:	Factors .... rate:
	age of marriage ....
	age of death ....
	therefore ....
Supporting ideas:	e.g. today:
	average age at marriage ....
	average age at death ....
	average length of marriage ....

E ⌷

Do you think Patrick speaks clearly? Can you say why?
  – Are the thought groups long or short?
  – Are the pauses frequent/infrequent? Long/short?
  – Does he emphasise focus words strongly?
  – Does his voice rise or fall at the end of ideas?

Listen to the recorded extract and write down exactly what you hear.
  Then go back and mark:
  – main pauses;
  – focus words;
  – pitch movement before pauses.

35   Student's dictation

In these last two units you can try to put what you have studied in this book into practice.

In this unit you will give a short dictation to other students and your teacher.

Dictation

Procedure

1 Choose a subject related to your profession or field of study and write three or four sentences about it.
2 Record the sentences on a tape recorder.
3 Prepare your audience, i.e. write any technical words that may be unfamiliar on the board.
4 Use the tape recorder to dictate the sentences to the class.
    a) Play the complete dictation once.
    b) Play it again pausing at the end of sentences (or where there are pauses).
5 The other students and teacher should write down the dictation. When they have finished ask someone to write their text on the board. At the same time, you write your own version on the board.
6 With the teacher's help, everyone should analyse the errors and misunderstandings.

Analysis

Compare the 'speaker version' and the 'listener versions'. Try and decide if missing or faulty words are due to the speaker's errors or the listener's errors. (If two or more listeners misunderstand the same word it is probably a speaker error.)

1 *Identify content words:* Content word errors (nouns, verbs, etc.) are far more important than structure word errors (articles, prepositions, etc.). For example, a noun mistaken for a verb is certain to make it hard for the listener to predict what is coming next.
2 *Circle focus words:* A long sentence will probably have more than one focus word. Missed focus words can cause major confusions.

3 *Check stressed syllables of focus words:* Make sure:
   a) the stress was on the right syllable;
   b) the sounds were accurate.
   Stressed syllables must be clear.
4 Are there any other possible sources of errors?

36 Student's oral presentation

In this unit you will give a short oral presentation to other students and your teacher.

Procedure

Each student should give a five-minute oral report on his or her field of interest. This talk must not be read from a script, but delivered from outline notes.

The rest of the class should take notes on the talk. If possible, the talk should be audio- or video-taped for feedback purposes.

The class and the teacher should then help the speaker analyse the clarity of the oral presentation, judging by the ease with which they could take notes from the talk.

Analysis

Use the 'Listener's checklist' from Unit 32 (page 126) to analyse each student's presentation.

1 DID THE SPEAKER MAKE IT EASY FOR THE LISTENER TO UNDERSTAND? (This is the essence of clear speech.)
2 *Amount of information:* Was there too much for a five-minute talk?
3 *Focus words:* Were they clearly pronounced?
4 *Thought groups:* Were they clearly marked?
5 *Pauses:* Were there enough pauses? Were they long enough (especially after new important information, e.g. technical terms)?
6 *Structure:* Was there an 'introduction', 'middle' and 'conclusion'? Was there a logical sequence to help the listener predict what might come next?

Further-study guide

When you finish this course it is important that you continue working on pronunciation yourself. Here are some suggestions to help you.

Pronunciation (PRODUCTION)

1 Make a note of your own pronunciation difficulties (elements that cause communication breakdown, e.g. word stress, sound contrasts, etc.) and try and concentrate on one of them at a time, for short periods.
2 Working with another student, record a few sentences for dictation (see Unit 35).
3 Listen to a short recording of natural speech, e.g. a song or part of the radio news. Try and mimic (copy exactly) the speech.

Pronunciation (RECOGNITION)

1 **Global**
   Listen to a recording of natural speech (15–20 seconds):
   a) Note any changes of subject/topic.
   b) Note all the focus words you hear (i.e. the most stressed word in a phrase/sentence).
   c) Note if the speaker uses long or short pauses.

2 **In detail**
   Listen to a very short extract of natural speech (5–10 seconds) and write it down as a dictation.

   Now, try some of the following:

   Sentence emphasis:
   a) Mark the focus words (see above).
   b) Mark the content words (i.e. words that contain important information; nouns, main verbs, adjectives, etc.).
   c) Mark the structure words (i.e. words that do not contain important information: articles, pronouns, auxiliary verbs, etc.).

⟫⟶

Elements of connected speech:
d) Mark contractions (i.e. missing letters/sounds, e.g. I have =
    I've).
e) Mark reductions (i.e. reduced sounds, e.g. 'Canáda').
f) Mark linking between words (e.g. 'when I arrived in Nice...').

Sound discrimination:
g) Mark all vowels with /ə/ sound.
h) Mark any disappearing letters (e.g. 'ta(l)k', '(k)now').